STFU

START THE F UP

STFU
START THE F UP

For Present and Future Leaders
of Startups, Small and Medium-
Sized Companies

RAJIVE DHAVAN

PARTRIDGE
A Penguin Random House Company

To order additional copies of this book, contact
Partridge India
000 800 10062 62
orders.india@partridgepublishing.com

www.partridgepublishing.com/india

Contents

To mom—you are still with me, and will always be.

To my dad and sister, who knew I was not happy with the usual definition of success; I wanted to look at failure, right in the eye! It is because of them I could make some crucial decisions in my life.

To my friends, who've been with me through thick and thin—they were extremely patient and understanding despite the fact that I missed a zillion occasions and milestones in their lives.

To J. Keith Murnighan, the author of many bestselling books, including *Do Nothing*—he's also been a distant teacher. His books and some interaction with him inspired me to pen something that would help new and budding entrepreneurs.

To some great visionaries and commendable entrepreneurs I had the opportunity to work and interact with

Introduction

This book is about a journey and not a destination. It is my way of looking at things. I have drawn my perspective from some fundamentals of business and management, self-belief, real-world experiences and failures. This is an attempt to bring you closer to a whole new way of looking at things, with an honest and a broader perspective—a perspective that lived deep inside you but never came to surface. This is an attempt to bring you closer to . . . you.

This book is not a guide to run your organization. It is certainly not about giving solutions to all the problems that you would face during your entrepreneurial journey; it is about inspiring you to look for solutions yourself. It is about empowering you to make the right decision.

The idea is to share with you some basic ideologies that I developed through the initial phase of my journey as an entrepreneur; no doubt I've got a long way to go. But the idea was to document a path that was recently treaded. It is for those who are in a similar situation in their professional life too. But it is also for some who've moved way higher but have been blinded on their way up.

It is not necessary that the solutions and situations mentioned in this book will fit your bill. But it would certainly take you a few steps closer to what you need. Entrepreneurship, to a great degree, is about being practical. Furthermore, practicality is not about aping this book blindly. It is about trying to get to the crux of various topics featured here. The bottom line is that the situations and problems faced by every leader are rarely identical; there will always be some aspects that are distinct to your situation, just the way it is rare to see two people think or behave alike. And perhaps, the goodness of the world is in retaining that difference to a certain degree.

But as leaders, you do not have the luxury of being the way you might want to be. You'll need to mould yourself. You'll need to create a structure of management that revolves around your people, and not you. You will need to live by an example. Remember that every time there is a crisis, we look up. That's how it works in organizations too. Of course, it is great to empower your people and make yourself redundant. But that takes time and a combination of right people. Until then, you can't be setting a symphony for your people and nudging the chords yourself.

Entrepreneurship is a tricky subject. Ironically, even though it doesn't have any shortcuts, we spend our entire life in search of one. As an entrepreneur, a leader, you ought to believe that in business, there is no such thing as 'one size fits all'. Everything is case-specific and erratic. Hence, you'll need to depend heavily on that one person who'll always come to your rescue—you! Yes, nothing helps you . . . like you!

1) Start—up or down. Why?

A good beginning is half done.
A bad one is all done.

The start-up culture in the world has grown by leaps and bounds in the last few years. The ecosystem is bustling with ideas, pitches, funding, and more. Start-ups have suddenly become the new in-thing. There was a time when people used to struggle to hire people for their start-ups. That's because employees understood the uncertainties and challenges that came along. They knew that there was no such thing as 'out of my scope of work'. The situation is still the same. But some start-ups have managed to showcase herculean growth. And that's added a lot of confidence in the to-be employees of a start-up. People today are not as sceptical to join a start-up. In fact,

Rajive Dhavan

there's a league of talent that wants to work with start-ups only. They realize that it is the best place to nurture their skills. But the flip side is that this has also given birth to a lot of *fauxtrepreneurs*. Well, that's a term coined specially for those who just keep talking about entrepreneurship but never really execute their ideas. These are the guys who talk about taking the big leap and starting something of their own. Well, the only reason they've not done that yet is because they're waiting for the 'right time'. From being smitten by some successful entrepreneurs around them to finding it plainly fascinating to be their own boss, the reasons could be many. But there's one question that every to-be entrepreneur needs to ask himself: Why start?

It is a very simple question. But it is the most difficult one to answer. And those who manage to successfully answer this one are definitely on the right path. The reasons for one to start could be many. But there are only a few that will actually help them through their erratic journey of entrepreneurship. So, what could be some good reasons for one to begin? Well, here are a few. Yours could be away from these. But as long as it is as valid as one of these, you'll certainly be a step closer to realizing your dreams.

1) Start only if you are truly *passionate* about your venture. Initial excitement about concepts, ideas, pitches, plans, et al. is great. But you'll soon run out of fuel if you

2

are not very passionate about your idea. Passion is the only fuel that will take you through all the tough times that you may face. It will make sure that your enthusiasm doesn't drop when things tend to go bad.

2) Move ahead if *money* is not the top reason for you to start that venture. Most people think that start-ups would soon start making money—in fact, a lot more money than they were earning as an employee. They get this idea from the numbers that they would have put down in their business plan. And when their business doesn't meet the expected numbers in time, they give up. Every organization has to make money. That's how it will survive and grow. But when just money becomes the focus, the product or service takes a hit. Most importantly, it affects the zeal with which one began their journey. That's when innovation drops. And an organization is reduced to sheer numbers. And with time, these numbers drop too.

3) Contrary to popular belief, you should try your hand at something when people warn you against it. There's no such thing as a safe start-up. If you can't *risk* it, don't even think of it. This is dedicated to all those wannabe entrepreneurs who have been employees for years. These are the guys who feel that they are entrepreneurs from within. They 'think' they have a great idea. They have the 'perfect' business plan. They

have 'enough' experience along with the 'required' potential. All they need is money. But before they take the plunge into the world of entrepreneurship, they just want to earn enough money that would take care of their expenses for some time, say, a decade. Once they have collected 'enough' money, they'd pitch their idea to investors. And the first investor they'll pitch their idea to will jump out of his seat and get set to invest in their venture. That's when it will be the best time for them to say goodbye to their existing job. Well, these are the kind of people who never really start. And that's actually best for them and the world both.

4) Ready to think beyond statistics? Statistics is a scientific way of doing business. But some of the most successful entrepreneurs will swear by the word *instincts*. Numbers are tricky. We always chase them. But they tend to find a way out. They somehow know which route we are taking to hunt them down. And they always find the other route to escape. This chase is an ongoing process for entrepreneurs though. But we have to give in to the fact that numbers are smarter. And there's only way to beat them. It is by listening to our instincts *(more on instinct later)*. If all entrepreneurs would just go by the numbers and not listen to their instincts, the world would have been short of so many great leaders and brands.

5) A start-up is more like a question bank. You'll have way too many unique situations to deal with. It is good to look for answers in books, online avenues, friends, and mentors. But if need be, you should be ready to get your hands dirty. You should be ready to *explore*. If you are planning to get into a business but not jump into it, you are wasting your time.

These are some answers to the question why should one even start in the first place. Some of these answers also talk about things one should stay away from. Whatever is your reason to take up entrepreneurship, just make sure that you get the bottom line right. And once you do, you'll know that you are ready to fly. But wait . . .

2) You are ready. Are they?

Entrepreneurship is a lot about teamwork. Sometimes, even before we hire a team!

Entrepreneurship is not a part of life; it is a way of life. When we begin our entrepreneurial journey, it is the idea that drives us. If we truly believe in the idea, we'll go that extra mile to make things happen. If the idea is more about just making money, we'll give up when we don't make money. And in the initial phase, more often than not, start-ups don't make a lot of money. So, those who aim for money only mostly get filtered in this stage. Others move ahead. We believe that we have to have a good hang of things to make a business successful. Well, that's true. But it is not enough. We think that our passion will drive us ahead towards daylight. Well, that's true as well. But it is not enough. Then there's hard work that will always come to our rescue. Even that's true. But yeah, it is not enough. Some heavy-duty words like perseverance, planning, hunger, and many more will begin to resonate. They will all help us gain confidence. But they won't suffice. That's because a start-up is our extension. It extends beyond us. Its strong traces are seen on people around us too, our friends and family for instance. Sometimes, we are ready but we forget to understand whether people around us are ready or not. But does that really matter? It does. It is not possible to work in extreme seclusion. Yes. An entrepreneur needs some amount of madness to make things happen. But in a practical scenario, even the biggest entrepreneurs depend heavily on their support system. This could be their family, wife, friends, or partners. So, it always helps to understand and analyze if they are ready too!

It is not like things will come to a standstill if the world around is not ready. But if it is, it will be of great help, especially when you truly need them. The dream of starting a business is one of the best things that can happen to an individual. But in order to make this dream come true, people have lost everything they had—their past, their future, and in some cases, the dream as well. Our focus is always on moving towards the right path at the right speed. But sometimes, we get so engrossed in this dream of ours that we forget the most important thing in life—balance. Yes. It is this balance that keeps us grounded and sane. The world of entrepreneurship is tricky and difficult.

And by the time we realize the importance of maintaining this balance, it is too late. We trip by then. That's when we need a lot more support. But our journey from fall to rise doesn't just become difficult; it becomes lonely too. That's exactly why it helps to gauge if the world around us is ready for our entrepreneurial endeavour. It is not like you have to wait for the world to be ready for your journey. Neither does that mean you need the world to approve your endeavours. It just helps to make sure that your support system is in place. And you know where to go when you see that inevitable fall. Despite being the most important part of an entrepreneur's life, a support system is the most underrated subject—a subject that hides behind the bright limelight that falls on the entrepreneur himself.

There are some specific reasons why it always helps if our support system is ready too. Here are three of them:

Time becomes more precious than ever before

When we begin our entrepreneurial journey, we barely have any money to invest. Even if we do, we're extremely careful about it. We work in a lean fashion, and focus on cost-cutting. But what we invest in abundance, without even blinking an eyelid, is our time. That's when our time becomes more precious, especially for our support system. We're in this constant struggle and thoughts to finish every single task at hand. Even when we are with people we love, our brain is on the job. It is important to disconnect. And most of us learn to do that over a period of time. But initially, it is difficult to draw that thin line. So, it is always good to analyze if our support system is ready to make the sacrifice. Is it ready to part us with our madness called entrepreneurship? Well, if it is, you'll always have company on this path. You'll never feel lonely. And that will make a lot of difference when the time comes.

Events are skipped as the madness takes over

We expect our family and friends to understand our situation better than anyone else. But sometimes, even they don't find it valid to accept our situation of being unable to spend enough time with them. So, when we are caught in the hustle and bustle of bringing our dream to life, we skip those very important milestones in their lives. It is a difficult choice we make. It is like a choice between closing that very crucial game-changing project and attending a best friend's wedding. The decision of an entrepreneur is obvious. So, of the many roles that an entrepreneur plays, he has to choose then one he wants to continue playing. But when he's got the right support system, it will always respect the role he ends up choosing . . . almost always.

Well, because no one understands us better

When we begin our journey, we're ready to do every single thing that's in our control to make our dream a reality. We are ready to make any sacrifice to take our entrepreneurial journey ahead. We invest crazy hours without even realizing. We miss crucial milestones in the lives of people around us—especially those who truly care for us. But it is these people who understand us better than anyone else. And it is their invaluable support that comes into play in times of trouble.

So, a good support system that's truly ready for us to take that plunge into entrepreneurship, will always come to our rescue, and be a saviour. That's when we'll not have to look anywhere else apart from that one single target—entrepreneurship.

3) To found or co-found

If marriage is an institution,
entrepreneurship is a university.

To found or co-found is a million-dollar question. It's a question that rings in the head of every to-be entrepreneur, especially during a phase when they have a lot of doors shut on them. It is also the need of a to-be entrepreneur who knows his skills, and wants someone good to fill up the gaps. There could be many such situations that give rise to a thought of having a co-founder. But it is a confusing question. Having a co-founder would mean that the dream is divided by two or more. It also means that the achievements and results are divided too. And for those who spend most of their time scanning through the cash registers, a co-founder would mean divided profits. And the greedy ones could go on to think that having a co-founder would mean that the credit would also get divided. Co-founders, however, come with their share of positives too. A co-founder means double the zeal. It means double the strength. It means double the brains. In some cases, it means double the business too. From double the achievements to double the credit, a co-founder can play a key role in most of these areas. These percentages, however, could vary from business to business. They would also depend on the roles and understanding between those involved. But the crux is that a co-founder is like two sides of a coin. He's got his share of flaws. But he comes with some positives too.

A founder and a co-founder are more like a couple. They have their share of differences too. And like all couples, these differences will crop up more in the initial years. It's important for founders to spend time with each other. Understand the other person's taste, point of view, and strengths. But like every couple, they need to adjust and sacrifice where necessary. They'll need to forgive at times too. This is the only way to make sure that the marriage and business last. That's because the co-founders, like couples, have the option for a divorce too. And in most cases it turns out to be a dirty one. So, some amount of back-end work before taking the plunge always helps.

So, how important is it to have a co-founder? Is it really advisable to have one in the first place? And if we decide to look for a co-founder, how would we get the right one? Starting a business

STFU—Start the F Up

is no joke. And so is looking for the right co-founder. Well, a co-founder can make or break your dream. A co-founder is the first person to join your bandwagon. There is no sure-fire way to look for that perfect co-founder. But there are certain good practices that one can consider when looking for a co-founder.

Analyze strengths and weaknesses

Well, looking for a co-founder is easy. Looking for the right co-founder is difficult. There are web portals and communities that help connect founders with the perfect co-founder. But it's not as simple as that. Whatever could be your channel, you'll need to do your share of work to get to the right person. And this could take longer than you think. So, be patient. An analysis of your strengths and weaknesses in the beginning will be of big help. Look for those who add value to the bigger picture. As leaders, we mostly end up connecting with people who are like us—these could be employees or co-founders. But the ones who fill in the gaps for our weaknesses are the ones that should be preferred. These are the ones who will add value to your dream in the real sense.

Look for someone with a history

When it comes to looking for a co-founder, consider the love marriage route. It's always best to know the person beforehand. It's always best to have a history with them. What's even better is if you've experienced the other side of the prospective co-founder. Yes. We all have that other side to us. It comes to the fore when things don't go as per our plans. It comes to the fore when our ideologies are challenged. It could be anger for some, anxiety for others. But if you've witnessed that side of your prospective co-founder, there is nothing like it. It's not necessary that you should be really thick friends with the prospective co-founder. But if you do have some decent information about them, and have interacted with them on a more personal level, it's a great beginning. And during this phase, if you've been exposed to that other side, it will give you a lot more confidence to move ahead in the right direction.

Set right expectations

Whether it's a marriage partner or a co-founder, setting right expectations is the best thing to do. It's also one of the most important things to do. Be vocal about what you expect from each other. And give it your best shot to live up to the other person's expectations. The issue with expectations is that, like creativity, they are subjective in nature. What seems a normal reaction to you might seem an abnormal one to the other person. So look for clear examples while setting the expectations. With the help of a little bit of paraphrasing, by hearing the crux of your expectations from the other person, you'll go a long way.

Be transparent, always

One of the biggest reasons for founders to part ways is transparency. When founders are not transparent to each other, they loudly convey wrong intent. Not being transparent leads to breaking the trust that the other person has placed in you. And when trust breaks, it shatters those involved. It also defeats the idea of having a co-founder in the first place. In fact, it also defeats the idea of a dream and a vision. This transparency is not limited to cash transactions; it goes way beyond. It purely depends on your equation with the co-founder. So people like to keep track of the smallest things just to make sure they are updated with what's happening. So, they like to be aware of a decision that is being made from the company's perspective. These people don't really appreciate decisions that are made in isolation. And most importantly, they don't digest the decision when it is brought to their notice by a third person. They prefer to hear it from the horse's mouth. So, whatever is the reason, being transparent with your co-founder, and vice versa, is highly important.

Give due credit

Like failure, success is an equally difficult thing to handle. Not many people can handle success with the right attitude. This reflects on their behaviour, and affects people around them. This is when people tend to think that they are solely responsible for all the success. And they begin taking all the credit for it. Money is important to most of us, but recognition is important to all of us. And when this recognition, in the form of credit, begins to slip from our hands, we tend to disconnect. The space between founders begins to increase. They no longer remain one strong force. This doesn't mean that credit should be given for every achievement. But where it's due, one has to give credit to not just the co-founder but the team as well.

Avoid close friends or family

As close friends or family, we tend to be lenient with each other. There's some amount of complacency that seeps in. But entrepreneurship is a serious business. So, unless you're sure that the friend or the family member has got the right sync with you, stay off them. Consider them only if you share a great equation with them, and you are sure that even if there's a disagreement in the future, you could sort it out, in an amicable fashion. It would be best if you've had your share of disagreements and fights with them in the past. Analyze how you managed to leave such things behind. If it was more of an easy patch-up, without any hang-ups, it's a great sign. If it was a highly dramatic one, you've got your answer.

So, ultimately, it is a great idea to look for a co-founder. But what is more important is to look for the right one. The idea is to make sure that the co-founder is able to add enough value to your venture. There could be options of involving co-founders or partners who would just be of monetary help. But always prefer the ones who can contribute in terms of skill. It's rare to find the right skilled people. And when you do find them, seal a deal with them. In any case, never rush into making this decision. If required, meet more people and try to gather as much information about them as possible. Like marriage, it's more of a long-term commitment. Make sure that you connect with those who understand and value your vision. Look for those who share the same zeal as you do. A co-founder is not a bad direction, just that the path is difficult. When you sense that you've hit a bump, make sure that the discussion is between you and your co-passenger—the co-founder—only. Respect the time and effort that has been put into bringing your venture to life. And if the time comes to part ways, don't rush into making a call. Sometimes, there's more than meets the eye.

4) What type are you?

Our style is influenced by the decisions we make.
But our decisions should not be influenced by our style.

Entrepreneurship, like a lot of other things in life, is highly influenced by style. It's the style of the leader. It is the man on top who leaves a lasting impression on not just his peers and employees, but his friends and investors too. How he leads, and what his style of entrepreneurship is are some questions that lead to defining him. He is identified that way. We've all got our natural styles of leading. But with time, we tend to mould ourselves. Obviously, it is in the interest of our company. But what we convey in terms of our entrepreneurship style is sometimes a well-planned strategy. Sometimes, it's more of a natural involuntary impact we end up creating. Whether it's planned or unplanned, it does help people classify us. It does speak volumes about our way of doing business and leading, both. In fact, it reflects in the product or services we offer, as well. It leads the way towards the kind of growth and innovation we'd like to embrace.

We've all got our own take on this heavy-duty subject called entrepreneurship. We all have our own ways of analyzing situations and making decisions. We've all got a distinct style of entrepreneurship. This style is what categorizes us into a specific type of entrepreneur. This distinct style of ours is not just restricted to us. It also rubs off on people around us: from co-founder to employees, from peers to mentees. The type of entrepreneurs also differs from one writer to the other. The way they categorize and describe a particular style of entrepreneurship is as varied as it can get. But there are a few commonalities in each one of these. In fact, there are many entrepreneurs who have no clue about what type they are. Perhaps it is a subject they don't focus much on. Or it could also be a difficult thing for them to observe for themselves and figure this out. But when all is said and done, there are styles and every style is unique. Most importantly, a leader's style could have a very heavy impact on the organization. This impact could be negative or positive. It purely depends on the leader, the entrepreneur. Sometimes the style of the leader overshadows the achievements of the organization too. And sometimes, it's the organization that takes away all the limelight, hardly leaving anything for the leader. Over the last few decades, leaders have become more conscious and aware of their style of leadership. In fact, a lot of them end up making some crucial decisions to carve this style of theirs. Some are naturals, whereas others work their ass off to highlight their style. But does having a distinct style of leadership really matter? Well, it does, to a great degree. Here are a few styles and what they bring to the table—good, bad, ugly, or sad.

The Aggressor

We've all got our own style to lead. Some of us are aggressive entrepreneurs, more like heavy or high-risk gamblers. Sometimes, it's not just risk but their stakes are pretty high too. They like to play the no-holds-barred game. These are the first movers—the attackers of sorts. They don't waste time in evaluating the result. Their only objective is to not give the person on the other side of the table the time to think or react. They are fierce, they are quick, they are bold, and they are loud. But it's this speed that ends up putting them in a tight spot more often than not. They move ahead with an unclear objective. Their only goal is to keep moving ahead. They get hurt in the process. They see a lot of damage happening. But all that doesn't affect them. They rarely introspect. And they just are known to move ahead. Their achievements are lesser comparatively. And that's never a bone of contention for them. They have a specific style of speed. And they love to magnify that with every passing moment. They leave the outcome or the result for another day.

The Thinker

Then there are the thinkers, who don't really focus much on the risk aspect initially. They invest a lot of time in just thinking. However, once they make up their mind, they make a quick call. Their evaluation of risk is pretty deep. That's because they don't just evaluate risk; they think deep about the broader picture too. The amount of time they take to react is more. But once they make up their mind and reach a conclusion, the speed with which they react is high. They gamble too. But their stakes vary. Once they are done looking at the bigger picture, they narrow down. They then focus fully on the risk factor. They work with a lot of permutations and combinations. They have a very clear objective. And that's how they know when to play the high-stake high-risk game, and when to quietly discard their cards. They always wait for the right moment to strike. They come across as slow because they mostly work in the back end. When the world thinks that they are actually not doing anything, they have a clear plan in the making. They are always on the game. They aren't bold. But they are smart. They are calm and composed yet unpredictable at times. But unlike the aggressor, when they trip, they take more time to put themselves back together. And that's why they end up losing a good opportunity at times.

The Pit Stopper

Pit stoppers do come across as the result-oriented type. But they rarely reach their destination. They are quick to react and start. They are highly enthusiastic. But their zeal doesn't last long, and tends to confuse the journey with the destination. They are great beginners. But their end is mostly unpredictable. They rarely have a clue about where they will land up. They are mostly at the mercy of good luck only. They don't really care about the process. It is something that they pick up from the 'aggressor'. That's because it helps them gain enough speed and momentum, at least in the beginning. Their focus on the path is hazy. They are unsure of what route to take. But they are clear about their destination. That's because for them, the destination is the pit stop. They think that reaching the pit stop is a great deal. And once they reach the pit stop, they can think about their next move. Their stakes are mostly high, and so are their disappointments. That's because they rarely reach their ultimate destination. They mostly just end up reaching midway. They hardly plan. At times, they tend to get ruthless in order to get to the pit stop though. They are overconfident. And that ends up becoming their biggest challenge.

The Dreamer

Entrepreneurship is all about dreams. In fact, dreams give rise to an entrepreneur's vision to begin. It is this dream that helps him make the most difficult calls of his life. It is this dream that he works towards to make it a reality. And the satisfaction he gets from seeing his dream translating into a vision and his vision translating into reality is enormous. But then there is a category of entrepreneurs who just dream. They execute less. Their stakes are high and so is their risk. That's because they mostly dream to win. But they rarely do. In other words, these are the ones who talk about aiming for some of the biggest goals, but end up achieving very little. Their optimum ability is restricted because of them living in a world of dreams. They don't really get a reality check. They think that a dream is all it takes to keep things rolling. Their risk-taking ability, however, is high. In order to make their dreams a reality, they make some bold moves. Most of these moves, however, are just a part of their talk only. They live in deep fear; the fear of losing. And that's exactly why they don't let their dreams burst. They see all the hurdles very clearly. But they refuse to accept them. They put people around them in unreasonable pressure. And this pressure begins to backfire. Slowly, they start seeing huge retaliation around them. They end up failing. And when they fall, they don't really get up. Ironically, their biggest enemy is their success. If they do succeed a little, they end up believing in their unrealistic dreams a lot more. They end up living under even more pressure from the society. They like to present themselves as larger than life, just like their dreams. And they soon end up becoming hollow from within.

The Finisher

The executioners are fierce like the 'aggressor'. But they also know when to be calm like the thinker. They plan. They work with a clear process and objective in mind. They are highly calculative. Their risk-taking appetite is very low. But they are consistently successful in their endeavours. They don't go larger than life. They know their limits, their game, and their playground. They know when to call it quits. They don't assume. They look to meet smaller goals. They dream less. But they know the value of results. They promise less but deliver as much. Their scale is small and they are pretty balanced in their approach. They take their time to think. But they don't think as much as a thinker. They react swiftly and move at a high speed, but not as swiftly as an 'aggressor'. They are confident. They bluff, they show, they do it all. They know the strength of their cards. And they know what they are good at. They are more in control of the situation. But this control leads to no innovation at all. Their attitude is more content and that's why they are not the high-flyers. For them, the bigger picture matters as much as the finer details. They do fail, and get up in a process that they feel is right. They learn from experience and mistakes. They don't take the big plunge. But they make their share of small gambles, at regular intervals. They are an interesting blend of various types. And their style is pretty predictable.

The X Type

We've spoken about how distinct each entrepreneur is. We have discussed in detail about the style of leadership that various leaders reflect. We have seen how this style of theirs impacts situations, people, and growth around them. But what we've not discussed is that not everyone can be categorized. There is an X type too. And that sixth type could be you. Well, the X type could be a unique combination of various types listed above. It could also be a completely different type away from the ones that have been listed above. One of their special qualities, however, is their ability to move away from their usual self, and make a decision. But the X type does exist. It's when no type fits. In fact, it could also be a type that changed over a period of time. It could be a rebel turned calm; it could be smart turned desperate. Or it could just be you.

5) Wrongly ethical or unethically right

A business without ethics is like a woman without substance; both live a lie!"

This is perhaps a very philosophical or a preachy point of view to share. But it is an area that's slowly fading away with time. It is because brands and leaders are running after creating wealth like never before. In a competitive world, wealth creation is certainly one of the most important tools to survive the ruthless attack of the market, competition, or time. But when ethics sink in the process, they take businesses along. A subject like business ethics is less spoken about. It is less written about too. But every successful entrepreneur knows the value of this word. They have all, at a certain stage in their lives, displayed unmatched business ethics that made them not just successful but earned the respect of their customers too. Then why is it that this subject is still virgin when it comes to speaking about it out in the open? Perhaps, it is assumed that every entrepreneur understands its value, and sticks to it.

There's a definition of business that has been doing the rounds for ages. A business is a result of the relentless work, planning, vision, and skill of a leader along with a team that he puts together, all this complemented by a great product or service that people would love to pay for.

For donkey's years, we've heard business leaders talk about how strategies have helped them float, how branding has been a great support system, how investors have been a boon to them, how their vision could drive the workforce, how their academics came into play, how their experience taught them things the hard way, how a mentor was a pillar of strength, how a zillion other things in the world were responsible for them running a successful business for decades. Though most of these factors count when building your business, there's one thing that, if missed, could ruin everything else—ethics!

History has given us loads of examples on how certain businesses soared great heights, and then suddenly went off the radar. A business owner's intent is what sets the ball rolling. It is said that a business leader—an entrepreneur—should not be emotional while making those tough decisions. But there's a thin line between being emotional and not choosing to be humane. Not everything in business is a robotic transaction. Sometimes, one needs to look at the world beyond deals too. Whether it is people who work for the organization, vendors who externally support the organization, or customers who are the prime reason for the existence of an organization, every segment counts and is as important as the other. There will always be times when a leader has to make difficult calls leaving all emotions behind, especially if this call is in the interest of the organization. But it works a great deal when these calls are less ruthless in nature. This could range from firing an underperforming employee to parting ways with an overcharging vendor. This could also include a client who's been a bad paymaster, for instance. Whatever the segment, a small consideration in a humane fashion always goes a long way in terms of building a truly respectable brand!

Remember, a brand is what customers say about it, behind the leader. A brand or a company is not very different from people. Like people, it has a personality of its own. It has its own way of communicating and reacting to various situations. It makes mistakes too. But like humans, it learns too. It grows with time. It moves ahead with experiences. But it becomes uptight in the process. It begins to live in fear, sometimes. And that's exactly why, when it goes wrong somewhere, it becomes all the more difficult for it to accept, more so when this acceptance is public in nature.

That's one of the reasons we see some big brands always trying to cover up their grey areas. Even when these areas are exposed to people, and everyone is aware of what's cooking, they try to play safe. But sometimes, a clear message of acceptance reassures a customer that the company is listening to them.

People run a business, and after years of ruthlessly doing so, they manage to scale up a bit. This gives rise to an incorrect impression that growth is being reflected. Well, maybe it is. But that's limited to the books of accounts only. Yes, a good-looking balance sheet is a delight for entrepreneurs, investors, et al. But because a brand is an intangible asset, we tend to put it on the back burner. As we move up the ladder, we love numbers more than anything else. A brand is not just a result of communication, branding, and perception. It is a lot more than that. The empathy that a brand shows, at times, adds to its personality. It increases its perceived value and makes it more loved than ever before. And when this empathy arises from an undertone of ethics, it will surely make a huge positive difference to the business and the brand both.

But it is easier to slip in the beginning of a journey. That's when the roads are more slippery. And the experience is less. That's when one seems to explore more shortcuts to reach the destination, and begins to see a zillion opportunities to give in to the temptation of always playing the game to his advantage. But the beginning of a journey is always more important than the rest of the journey. And a little balance at that stage always works wonders.

The right intent always keeps the fire of scaling greater heights burning. It is a great reminder to make sure that innovation should be looked at seriously. It always helps in creating an organization, a brand that's beyond the leader. It gives rise to an organization that thrives on the right value-system. It helps in gaining more loyal customers—internally and externally both. It keeps the sheer reason for an organization's existence alive.

When the intent goes wrong and ethics sink, businesses begin to fall like a pack of cards, leaving only traces of some bad taste behind. Well, the fact of the matter, however, is that ethics can't be taught. They should be a natural part of an entrepreneur's journey. And even if they can't be taught, they can always be reminded and reiterated!

6) Ineffective communication affects

When you talk, you give others a piece of your mind.
When you communicate, you help them understand it.

Like entrepreneurship, communication is an art too. It can, however, be mastered over a period of time. All it needs is continuous practice. But when we talk about communication, people think it's more to do with the English language. Well, it is. And that's because English is a widely used common language across cultures, countries, and companies. But that's not all. There's a lot more to communication than that. It's certainly one of the most underplayed subjects. We don't

31

discuss much about them because we assume that most leaders are good at communication. Yes, they are. And that is one of the reasons why they are where they are. From Steve Jobs to Bill Gates, Mark Zuckerberg to Richard Branson, every leader has got his distinct style of communication. And that style is not restricted to the English language. It's way beyond just that. These leaders know how to put their point across in the best possible way. They know what we call the art of effective communication. They know how to influence. They know how to get the desired answers. Most importantly, they know how to get their share of attention. Apart from their technical or entrepreneurial genius, it's their style of effective communication that makes them what they are.

There's no dearth of great talent in the world. But most of the leaders in the making lose the race just because they don't know how to start a business meeting, or give a proper speech, or write an effective email. They don't know how to effectively communicate and influence to win. The reason for most of them failing could be as simple as poor communication. They don't know how to structure their thoughts. Despite being technically strong, and having all those qualities that a great leader possesses, they end up failing. And sometimes it's just because they come across as highly doubtful and confused. The best investment a leader or an entrepreneur can make is to invest in oneself, apart from his team though. Whether it comes down to getting the basics of language right, or perfecting the art of business writing, nothing should stop one. A tool as simple as an email can do wonders if it's written well. The structure of the message, the introduction, and the end—all aspects should finely blend together. They should, at least collectively, not leave any doubts in the minds of the readers. Communication plays such a major role that when it is ineffective it leads to low self-confidence. And when the confidence is low, the leader will not be able to get the much-needed attention of his employees or his client. And that is a sure-fire recipe for failure.

But communication is not as complicated a process as it seems. It can certainly be broken down into very simple steps to get the basics right. Of course, these steps are not enough to create that distinct style of your own. But they should suffice to help you save your company's face when it is needed the most. They will help you take charge of the situation if need be. They will make sure that you are ready to take that life-changing meeting, or send that most important email, with enough confidence. Finally, they will help you with that transition from getting your basics right to creating your own distinct style, just like the icons you admire today. But all this will be possible only when you take that first step and practice. These are indicative in nature. So, you can always add your own flavour to these, and come up with your own version.

Begin with confusion

Yes, you read that right. We all learn a few things with experience. Sometimes, we end up thinking that we are doing things wrong, just because we compare our beginning with someone else's middle or end. Some of the best leaders have also taken time to master the art of effective communication. Some of us do have a natural knack for communication. But most of us struggle, especially in the beginning. But we don't struggle because we are weak in this area or it's new to us. We struggle because of this big demon called confusion. We don't know where to start, what to write, or what to say. We pause the moment we meet this demon. It puts a full stop to all our energy to move ahead. But who said confusion is a negative thing? It's not. We all get confused with things. We all are surrounded with a zillion thoughts. And we all go through that phase where we don't know how to put our thoughts down. So, confusion is not a bad beginning. In fact, it just means that we are normal. And we can look at doing things the normal way. We need to get rid of this impression that with the kind of clash of thoughts that is going on in our head, it is impossible to get clarity. Well, it is possible. Accept confusion. Let it take over you. Don't resist. The more you resist, the more it defeats the whole purpose. Use this time to calm down your head. Use it to breathe deep, and take the next step.

Have a clear objective

Yes, it's good to start from the end. When you are writing an email or giving a speech, it's important to have clarity as to what your ultimate goal with that action is. This could be as simple as just impressing people and leaving them with a thought. Whatever the objective is, make sure you know it. When you know your destination well, you'll not just find the best way to reach there, you will also know when you reach it. Shooting in the dark with no idea of what you want your audience to take away from your speech or the email will just take you nowhere. If it's an email, you should know what action you'd want the person on the other side to take. This way you will be able to clearly analyze those hits and misses. You can then evaluate and improvise too. An objective also helps in structuring the rest of the communication effectively.

Research before you write

This is a very simple thing to do. But most of us skip this. Whether it's an email or a speech, unless you have your facts right, you will not sound confident. And if you don't sound confident, you will not be able to influence your audience. Worse still, you will not get their attention. Business is a game of trust. An employee works hard to gain the trust of his employer. A prospect works hard to gain the trust of the interviewer. A leader works hard to gain the trust of his clients. The leader also works hard to gain the trust of his people, his team, or his employees. It's like a cycle—a continuous process. And a good part of this trust depends on how confidently we convey our thoughts. How honest we are while conveying those thoughts. Also, whether our thoughts are based on research or not. So, there is a lot that depends on research. Sometimes, even if we are sure about the subject, spending a few minutes before we write or speak always comes in handy. Remember, with time, facts change too. What was a fact yesterday could become a rumour tomorrow. And what is a rumour today could become a fact tomorrow. So, stay updated with the subject that you intend to speak or write about.

Write down key points

Yes, write down. Even if you are a pro, it's always good to just write down some key points. Writing down is the simplest technique to clear our thoughts and streamline them. These same thoughts, when they are moving around in your head, will remain unclear. But don't panic. Writing doesn't mean you have to be an established writer. Even if you are not the writer types, it's okay. One doesn't need to be a great writer to do some effective business writing, or communication, for that matter. Before you start writing that most crucial email, or before you start preparing for that really important meeting, just put down a few pointers together. These pointers will be the skeleton of your communication. Once you have this skeleton or structure ready, it will be easier for you to add all the required body mass to it. These pointers will also help the audience or the reader better understand what you are trying to convey. You will have your point of view put across clearly, and with way fewer hassles.

Don't forget to review

Some of the best writers in the world swear by this one. We all make mistakes. And a good review is the best way to reduce them. A good review, in fact, ends up being the big difference between a good writer and an average one. Some typos or grammatical mistakes in a write-up, email, or memo will give a very bad impression of not just the leader but the company too. If you've written an email late in the night, and it's not an urgent one, it is best to push it to the next morning. Of course, it needs to go through a round of review, before it is shot. Most of us have the habit of sending emails, contracts, memos, etc. without reviewing them. And all the mistakes end up conveying that we are not serious about what we have written. Imagine a prospective employee who comes to see you with his résumé, and you find a couple of grammatical mistakes on it. Would you really want to hire him? The prospect could be great at his core skills. But with a résumé like this, at least once you'll have your share of doubts on his seriousness towards your company and the job. It's pretty similar when you do that in your written communication with clients, investors, or employees.

In simple terms, all you have to do is define, write, research, and review. This quick process will help you fix the flaws in your communication, and convey your point of view better. It will help you become more confident. Most importantly, it will guide you towards a self-learning direction. That's because learning about communication can take a lifetime. There will always be scope for improvement. And with every step towards improvement, you will speak better, write better, and influence better.

7) Use emails as if they were paid

The difference between use and misuse is similar to the difference between fee and free.

   Communication plays an important role in the success of every business. That's exactly why a lot of companies formulate and stress practicing on the guidelines they set for internal and external communication. Right from the kind of company font that is to be used, to the structure of communication that is pre-formatted for various situations. This purely to enhance the way the complete organization communicates internally and externally. It is also to standardize all communication as if it were being done by one single brand. It is a great practice to follow. It does reassure the end customer and show the brand in a good light. There are debates over how brands have robotized the way they communicate with end customers, but that's another issue altogether. However, in every form of communication, personalization works great—more so in written communication. That's because a written form of communication has more chances of being misinterpreted. So, it is imperative to make sure every single word is carefully chosen. But in a fast-paced world where every minute technology evolves, it is difficult to not make it a part of our working culture, especially if this technology is *free*!

E-mail communication has become one of the most commonly used modes of official communication. Or should we say most commonly misused mode of communication? In fact, it is so common that we've forgotten the times when it was a luxury to be able to send and receive an email. There used to be one computer in an office. And people would wait with bated breath anticipating an important email. But like they say, anything in excess is harmful. And today, that's what email is doing to organizations that don't really understand how this mode of communication should be used.

Email writing is a skill. In fact, there are many businesses that don't see the light of the day because of the representative's inability to write one.

In a small set-up, emails tend to be a big hindrance in clear communication—something that every start-up, or even a bigger company, for that matter, depends on. More often than not, we tend to exchange emails a lot more than actually required. And because of this excessive use, various app developers saw a problem area in us not being able to manage our inboxes. Though the solution works for some, it still can't take care of the issue, right from its roots. With the number of emails that we receive on a daily basis, we also miss seeing an empty inbox. In order to get a glimpse of one, we tend to pass on the tasks to others. All in all, an empty inbox ends up being nothing more than an illusion. So the question is, did we actually complete all our tasks, duties, or responsibilities? No.

This excessive use of technology leads to people exchanging emails even if they are working in a pair and in the same room. It is a disastrous waste of time, effort, and technology. Some leaders prefer working in smaller teams. And one of the key reasons for that is the ease of communication it brings. Fewer emails are exchanged and more work is executed. That's because emails tend to distort execution.

With time, however, emails will also become a thing of the past. With applications that are becoming a new internal communication channel for teams, companies are slowly taking this channel external too. And that too will be misused for being free, perhaps.

But the age-old face-to-face conversation is still way ahead of all this technology. That's how humans communicate naturally. There are times when emails help. But a simple analysis of where they are being overused will certainly save a lot of time and effort. And for a start-up, or even a bigger organization for that matter, time is of greater importance than even money.

Finally, a smarter way of using this mode of communication effectively is to use it as if it were paid.

8) Brand your brand right

It's easier to be the second someone.
What's difficult is to be the first you.

When we start or run a business, we get so involved in so many areas that we tend to take the most crucial aspect for granted—communication (advertising and branding). Whether it is a product or a service, the role of branding is way beyond what people normally perceive. For instance, a great product that's not promoted well will soon become extinct. The flip side, however, is that a bad product that's heavily promoted will vanish even faster! That reveals the importance of a brand, its promotional strategy, and the branding partner. A branding partner could be a full-fledged agency or a freelancer. Ultimately, it's the much-needed partner for your brand to come to life and sustain its communication efforts. But there are certain best practices that would help you connect better with any of these options that you may go ahead and zero in on. Remember that your uncle's techie son who is in the final year, is certainly not a good fit or example for a branding partner. Every single piece of communication and design needs experience and thought. There is a science behind how things should move ahead, at what pace, and in which process. For a businessman who's engrossed in his balance sheet, it could be a smart move to save some bucks. But from a brand owner's perspective, it is a move that could hamper his biggest asset—the brand.

It is important that you help your branding partner with as much information as possible. This information could be about your product or service and even the industry, for that matter. In case you are creating a new category and moving into a virgin territory, you'll need to give ten times more information to your branding partner. Once information is shared, try to evaluate their understanding. And once you are sure that the person or the company you've interacted with understands your vision, you will know that you are ready to roll. And if you reach a conclusion that they can execute your project and add life to your dream, seal a deal with them without any delay.

This, however, is only the beginning of your journey to put your brand together. The biggest hurdles are yet to show up. It is an art to get the best out of your branding partner, and not many people can do it successfully. But here are a few observations that will help you a great deal through this tedious process.

Involve, don't interfere

When you hire someone to do a job, you need to have faith in them. If you don't, your own skills of bringing them on board shall be questioned. To get the best out of your branding partner, it is very important to work in sync with them. However, sometimes we tend to forget that they know their job better. There is a very thin line between involvement and interference. And crossing that line would have implications on your brand. Remember, at the end of the day, your biggest asset is the brand—*your* brand!

Promote one thing at a time

It is a known fact that your audience's attention is short-lived. They are exposed to hundreds of pieces of communication every single day. With relentless hard work and a good team, it is possible for every communication to be out of the box. Despite this, what is more important is whether you get your share of attention for your communication or not. All you need to do is prioritize one key message or information you wish to share with your audience. It is time to declutter and focus on what you really need to say. Discuss this with your branding partner and they'd love to help you out with this.

Ego at bay, brand in sight

Ego is a sign of weakness. And building a brand is not for the weak-hearted. Only when your ego is at bay will your brand be in focus. Discuss, share, explore, but don't exploit. A branding company comprises creative and sensitive people, who are excited about the work they do. It is this excitement that keeps them going. They like to add value to your brand. Working with them as a team adds to their excitement, and it can take your business ahead, beyond what you can imagine. But when your ego overshadows everything else, including your brand, you'll soon be in a tight spot.

Comment vs. compliment

If you like something your branding partner has done, it always pays to be vocal about it. It is a known fact that creative people value honest appreciation more than anything else, even money at times. Nonetheless, we cannot deny the importance of feedback—constructive feedback. Picture this—if something goes wrong, don't you make a huge fuss over it? But what makes you think a zillion times before you share a few words of appreciation when something goes great? It is a myth that appreciation makes people complacent. In fact, it is a proven way to get the best out of your branding partner.

Dues can harm in due course

Your branding partner is a service provider, and it provides a very important service. Not clearing their dues on time doesn't give a good picture of your brand to them. As a branding partner is an extended arm of your business, it's safe to consider them as your own team, which means they are in the same league as your employees. Hence, they are your first and internal customers. So, not settling their dues on time would mean that you're creating a picture of disbelief in front of your initial and crucial customer. In the long run, this could be nothing short of a disaster for your business, though. As a business leader, it should be your personal responsibility to make sure that your first customers, your employees and vendors, get the hang of your vision first-hand, and they see some great chemistry with your brand. Only then they would stick around to help you scale. At the end of the day, every business needs money. And your branding partners are no different. By settling their dues on time, you are actually helping your own brand. This way they'll invest more time in developing your brand instead of following up with you for what you owe them. But if you don't live up to your commitment and settle them on time, what will occupy their minds more than your brand will be your outstanding dues. And this would soon reflect on your brand too.

Ready to brand your brand right?

These simple steps will take your business and association with the brand partner a long way. Every business needs great associations and partners that will help them survive ruthless volatile markets, and still make a difference. So, it is not that difficult to get the best out of your branding partner. Remember that nothing is built overnight. So, be patient and work closely with your branding partner, and remember that your brand's partner is not yours. So, keep unwanted tantrums aside. Then, get set to give your brand the edge that it truly deserves. Get set to brand your brand right!

9) Company culture is crap if . . .

If a leader doesn't set the right culture,
someone else will set a wrong one.

With a lot of difficulty we start that first venture of our life. Even the biggest entrepreneur would remember his early days. That's because it is those days that must have taught him the most. But a company is not about the entrepreneur only. It is also about people who work with him. It is about these soldiers who win the war with him. It is about the team that works as hard to help him realize his dream. And if there are people, there will be a culture that will be established over a period of time. This culture is nothing but a collective outlook that most people in an organization have. It is called company culture.

It is obviously not the only thing that describes the term *company culture* effectively. In fact, there are quite a few influential factors involved; from the way leaders manage their teams to the ideologies that are seeped deep inside them, everything matters. Perhaps the very reason HR (human resources) departments exist is to reiterate the fact that people should be of high priority to an organization. It is these people who come together to make or break the culture of a specific organization. They define the future of culture of any organization. So, it is important to make sure that the culture is aligned to your ideologies and beliefs as a leader. And that's because it is you who decided to take that first step towards being an entrepreneur. It is you who came up with the idea that would some day see the light of the day. It is you who had a lot more zeal than anybody else to execute, to lead, and to make this happen. And once it did happen, it is you who has to make sure that the company culture is just right.

Entrepreneurship can be tiresome. Start-ups can drain one of all the energy that one might have. In fact, we tend to use all our energy in improving the product or service we have to offer. History has shown us that the leaders played a key role in defining and polishing the culture of the companies they led. And this culture was their extension. The best example is the founder of Apple—Steve Jobs. He was known to be comfortable working with smaller teams. Also, the culture he promoted was more of his extended personality and belief.

A company can adopt any culture as long as the leader believes in it. Sometimes, a company can also have two cultures that coexist. It could be an aggressive set of people. This is more of a company that has a team of go-getters. These are people who are always on their toes. They are hungry, and want to achieve more. The culture of a company can also be a result-oriented one. This is more about executioners, those who don't linger around problems; they solve, they execute. This is a set of people that's driven to come up with conclusions. Apart from these, you can consider developing a culture that's beyond books and theories too. A company can be inclined towards innovation too. It is another known type of company culture though. In fact, it is also a highly attempted company culture. A company can have any culture. But along with that, every company wants to be innovative. Innovation needs perseverance. As an inventor, Thomas Alva Edison made over a thousand unsuccessful attempts at inventing the light bulb. So, an innovation culture can be achieved though promoting a culture that accepts failure. The fear of failure has to be completely removed. Only then innovation can prevail. And that's a different way of achieving innovation. Similarly, one can move way beyond the theoretical company cultures and define one's own.

Entrepreneurs don't really have to struggle hard to arrive at what should be the culture that their company should adopt. That's because this culture is more often than not an extension of a founder's vision, experiences, mission, and beliefs. All you have to do is ask yourself the right questions. Have clear answers. Put them down on paper. Evaluate them. Analyze them. And if you still believe in them, convey them to those who matter. But remember that a dominant or a primary company culture is of no use if it is either implemented incorrectly, or coexists with a subculture that doesn't complement it. Sometimes, despite defining the right culture, we fail. Well, that could be due to various reasons.

Company culture is crap if initial hires don't believe in it.
So, the very first hire is as important as the leader himself.

It is the initial people you hire who'll help you define a company culture. But more often than not, once you get more involved and engrossed in handling various tasks as a leader, company culture will take a back seat. That's when it is these initial hires that will help you keep it on an autopilot mode for time to come. Along with you, it is these initial hires that lay the foundation to a company culture that you'd like to have. In the midst of all the chaos that you'll go through while bringing to life your start-up dream, you could easily miss out on kick-starting the right company culture. And if the beginning of a company culture is not set, it'll become increasingly difficult for you to fix it as you move ahead. The best thing to do is to make sure your initial hires are aligned to the culture you prescribe. Brief them, train them, induct them; it is all going to be so damn worth the effort.

Company culture is crap if not implemented at the right time.
So, a lot depends on how a company begins its journey.

Sometimes, it is too late to define the culture of a company. If a leader doesn't focus on it in the beginning, the initial hires will end up defining one. And this could be a culture that suits them best. For instance, it could result in an individualist culture where people will tend to work in seclusion. Most businesses rely heavily on teamwork. And that could well go out of the window if the culture of a company is not set in the very beginning. Once the individualist culture is set by the initial hires, it will become extremely difficult for a leader to change it at a later stage. It becomes a norm, more like an unwritten rule that is followed by one and all. In fact, over a period of time, this culture becomes so strong that it remains even after the people who defined it leave the organization. It stays way beyond them. And it just continues to get stronger with time. By the time we realize, the damage is already done.

Company culture is crap if subcultures don't complement it.
So, setting the right primary culture is not where it ends.

A subculture is not something that can easily be avoided in an organization, more so in bigger organizations. Sometimes, it is beyond our control. A subculture is a culture that a part of a company adopts; this could be a specific team, process, or a business unit. It is not necessary that this is always harmful to a company. That's because a subculture can be something that complements the primary culture of a company too. For instance, a big company defines its company culture as a result-oriented one. Its focus is just on results. The outcome matters to it more than anything else. And it wants every employee to be a part of this culture and drive it. Well, a part of that company can have an aggressive subculture that perhaps could coexist with a result-oriented one. It is purely because aggression helps a big deal in achieving results. But when the subculture is in contrast with the company culture, and doesn't complement it, it can have adverse effects on not just the people but also goals of the company. A company, for example, could have a culture that's team oriented, a culture that promotes teamwork, a culture that expects teamwork. But if the subculture in the company is more inclined towards individualism, it defeats the purpose of the organization trying to create a dominant team-oriented culture in the first place. The individualist subculture focuses more on private life or personal economic gains when compared to teamwork that's more about the greater good of the team and the organization on the whole.

10) Can't hire the best? Extract it.

There are no best employees in the world.
The ones who were, are employers today.

Every successful entrepreneur who has spoken about hiring has always mentioned how important it is to hire people that are better than us. Leaders have stressed the fact that hiring people who've got more varied skills than ours will always impact the growth of an organization positively. So, hiring people that are different and better skilled is certainly a great route to take. But what's next? Well, most leaders think that it is the end of the game. More so, it's the newer lot that identifies with this thought.

Well, in today's times, an entrepreneur's knowledge base has to be so huge that he should possibly have enough information about all the aspects of his business. In a world that is so fast-paced, hiring differently is not enough. It is not a milestone. It is just a break to learn more. It is just an opportunity to use that time to firm up our know-how. An entrepreneur's life is not a limited period offer (LPO) or a happy-hour window at a food joint; it is his way of life. And this life demands learning to be of utmost importance. Even if you manage to hire people better than you, it is your core responsibility to not let them remain better than you. You have to work so hard on your skill that by the time you re-look at hiring, the bar you'd set for yourself should go up by a few notches.

But apart from hiring the best, there's another school of thought that says, 'It is not important to have the best team. What's important is to extract the best from your team!' When an entrepreneur begins his journey, it is this school of thought that will keep him going. In a scenario when a business is struggling to make both ends meet, this one seems like a more viable option.

So, how does one extract the best from an average team? Is it possible to get them to perform any better? These are some of the questions that start-up leaders are surrounded with. And that's because they know that all they can afford is an average employee—anything more than that is a bonus. Extracting the best from an average team is very difficult. But that's exactly why you, the leader, are at the helm of things.

The *right* kind of motivation goes a long way. The word *right* is stressed because every individual perceives motivation differently. It is good to assume that there are certain channels of motivation that everyone will appreciate. But again, assumptions don't transform start-ups, facts do! So find out what motivates your people, and move ahead accordingly.

A shared vision is one of the most underrated qualities of a leader. Leaders are known to be visionary. But how much of this so-called vision goes deep down the organization or the team? Well, the strength of a vision depends on the number of people who swear by it.

The third ingredient is personal gain. The difference between the right kind of motivation and personal gain is shelf life. Every individual would be interested in motivation that comes from the boss. But these things are less at shelf life when compared to a personal long-term gain that you could share with a team member, something that is custom-made to his aspirations, goals, career plans, growth, etc.

Apart from these, there are a couple more ingredients that can work their magic. But you'll have to explore these ingredients based on the situation, the person you are dealing with, and few other such influential factors.

With the right blend of these ingredients, you can whip out that perfect dish. But remember, you'll have to add salt to taste . . . not yours, that of the one you are dealing with.

You think it is that simple? No. There will be times when none of these would work. It happens with a lot of entrepreneurs out there. This is when you need to get back to the drawing table. And analyze that one thing which tops this list, or any other list—intent. Yes, if a leader is trying to persuade his team without basic integrity, and an intent that is negative, it shows. You could be the best actor in the world, but when you are not honest to your craft and your team, it shows. It always does. And that's when there's a need to fix yourself up first. Entrepreneurship is a slippery road. It is luring, it is addictive, it is blinding, and it is everything that can change the real you during the course of the game. But history is full of names of leaders who were honest with their craft. Every rags-to-riches story will have a couple of episodes where the protagonist would have gone off track, and would have been blinded. But it is only strong ethics that would have helped him get back to business. Intent is more like a cleaning agent. Before you whip up that dish, you'll need to clean every ingredient with positive intent. That's when you will know how to make the best use of the ingredients you have. And that's when your dish will taste great, *naturally*.

11) Only if processes could build people

If you've got more processes than required,
you'll need another process to monitor them.

A process, as per most companies, is the only right way of doing things. This could be adhering to certain guidelines, or following a specific set of instructions to perfectly complete a task. But who cares about these processes? These could be subject matter experts or trainers, if it is a technical process. If it is a non-technical official process, it could be the human resources or corporate communications department. And if it is a start-up, it is an individual who heads the company, and creates these processes. So, in most cases, processes are a result of an individual or a group of individuals' perspective. It is what one or a few think would be the best thing to do. It is more of an outcome from a few that needs to be followed by all. But why is it so difficult to involve the people in question to create a process that they'd actually love to follow? Why is it difficult to have an open mind that some processes don't liberate the executors, they end up limiting them? It is felt that the more the processes, the more things will be predictable. The more things are predictable, the more one will have control. Unfortunately, it is never the case. The reality in fact is that the more the number of processes, the weaker an organization gets.

So, it is never really about the number of processes. It is about the number of required processes.

Companies end up investing in extra resources and experts to develop processes that they think will fix all issues. And it becomes an ongoing process of creating and implementing new processes. These are the ones that do more harm than good. Well, what's the point of having a specific process when it is neither understood nor followed by those it was actually created for? Is creating a new process to tackle every new issue really the best way to go about it? Absolutely not!

But that doesn't mean processes are not important. It is not possible for a company to survive without processes either. The point here is to make sure that every process laid is relevant to the time, job profile, and culture of the organization. It should not be an extension of a group of individuals, or the fancy of a blinded leader. A process needs evaluation. Most big companies do that. But it is the start-ups that most face the issue of creating new processes for every new issue that they face. Imagine in the game of cricket, the captain calling for a field change with every single ball just because the batsman gets the better of the bowler. Well, a change in field is necessary. It needs to be done at the right time too. But if it is done at the drop of a hat, it just leads to sheer confusion amongst other players. It is more like even before players are used to one field positioning, they are asked to switch. This way they are not allowed to get comfortable and given the opportunity to perform.

One of the best things to do, however, is look for suggestions. Engagement works great in not just implementing a process but making sure it helps streamline and fix rough edges too. When a process is being set, try to get inputs from those it is being set for. Perhaps you'll get some relative insight that could make the process worth accepting. Blindly aping processes that have been doing the rounds for decades is never the best solution. Some basics never change. But the world beyond the basics is huge. It is erratic and unpredictable. Look for bespoke solutions that will ease out certain issues in reality, and not just on paper.

Some processes can come across as harsh to people they're aimed towards. These could come across as biased and unnecessary. But at the end of the day, the leader has to make certain calls that might not really go down well with all the employees. It is not like the leader can always focus on making sure he keeps everyone happy all the time. But getting inputs from some key people always helps, especially when it comes to processes that are perceived as harsh. Well, in such scenarios, it is best to design the process implementation in phases. Giving a decent heads-up to employees beforehand helps them be prepared for what's to come. It helps in easing out all the tension that revolves around these processes. It also gives time to the leader or the respective department heads to tweak the process where necessary. Incidentally, the perception of a process doesn't just depend on the people involved or those who it is being designed for. Sometimes, the perception depends on the experiences that the employees would have had in the past. It is a mindset they rarely drop. And it becomes even more difficult for a leader or a specific department head to execute these processes. But mostly, the ones who are affected the most by these so-called harsh processes are the ones who've spent maximum time in the organization. These are the senior employees who've been used to a certain way of functioning. And that becomes stronger with time. They expect the organization and the leaders to behave in a specific way. So, it becomes all the more difficult for them to cope with change. And when this change is a radical and a sudden one, it begins to raise questions in their mind. A relatively new employee, on the other hand, has fewer expectations, and a weaker state of mind. And it is comparatively easier for him to accept such radical changes. So, do focus on your key people—the ones who've been a part of the system for a long time, and the ones who hold various key roles in the organization. And then make sure the process smoothly slides down into the system with all the key people in the loop.

Creating a process, or even a policy, for that matter, is just a part of the whole strategy. Monitoring it is the real challenge. In fact, process monitoring is a critical area. It is the line between a successful process and the one that remains a mere source of mockery to the employees. Larger organizations have specific teams in place to monitor any deviation by the employees. And they have specific corrective action plans laid out too. Start-ups don't have the liberty to appoint special monitoring teams like their bigger counterparts. So, before every process is penned, the question of how it will be monitored should be asked. Apart from monitoring, the other key area is how a breach would be dealt with. Certain realistic examples with a plan of action would come in handy to the leader. And this would also reflect the seriousness of an organization to implement and benefit from the processes that are prescribed. Ultimately, it would lead to a win-win situation for the employees and the employer alike.

12) Sometimes all you have to do is stick around

Patience doesn't just mean wait.
It also means weigh.

When things start soaring in organizations, processes are tweaked, new roles are created, the crisis management team is called in, budgets are allocated, strategies are formed, board meetings take place, and a whole lot of hush is created to address the issue. People are forced to think for solutions that would fix the problems. Small businesses do not have the luxury of defined roles, excessive meetings, a huge set of board members, or the comfort of departments and teams that specialize in crisis management. These are more about one man's instinct that is an amalgamation of emotions wrapped in strategies, and hope wrapped in goals. In order to address every issue that crops up, entrepreneurs tend to forget the basics. Entrepreneurs tend to ignore the fact that sometimes we don't find solutions at that very moment. And that's not because we lack the required skills; it is because our approach is a forced one. It is more about coming out of the problem with a clean chit, quickly. We focus on fixing up what's at hand and forget the big picture in the process. The big picture is not about clearing that very episode; it is about understanding the crux of the problem better. And that happens only when we decide to stick around. With a natural tendency to face challenges, we forget to take that much-needed pause.

This pause is what we call the art of sticking around and doing nothing. That's because our mind needs free space to function better. When we're stuffed with a problem, there's no room for a solution to show up. These are the times when all you need to do is stick around. You don't have to move ahead, you don't have to prove that you are on the job, you don't have to answer, you don't have to question; all you have to do is take a pause. That's when you'll really see things from a broader perspective. That's when you you'll not just discover solutions, you'll begin to create them.

One such instance took place in one of the biggest e-commerce companies. It was a team of 250 people who were handling one of the most complicated areas of business—premium customer complaints. There was a sudden and an unusual rise in customer complaints. As this was an important aspect of the business, it was very evident that the team was struggling. All the frills of the big and heady organizations came into play: senior management's advice, team leaders' involvement (read 'interference'), communications team's intervention, et al. Every single person had his own understanding of the situation and its adverse affects on the business.

Now was the time when everyone wanted to work out a solution and take credit for the radical change they could strategize to bring the situation under control. The reason for the downfall was identified as the recent new hires who were inducted into the team. It was said that these individuals lacked the skills required to be a part of the team. They were, apparently, not trained properly. There were other obvious reasons that were identified too. And then began all the retraining processes, customer-centricity initiatives, performance-linked incentive plans, and a few more steps that would bring about the required change. Nothing worked!

The reason was simple; the real problem was never identified. All the solutions were being worked around imaginary problems that were built on the fancy of each individual who had a say. So, what really went wrong?

Well, there was a technology failure. The software went a bit haywire. Instead of showing the data of customers who had to be contacted today, it reflected the data of customers who had been contacted the previous day. It was obvious that the customers were irate because of the repeated attempts to reach them. They were annoyed with the fact that their previous commitment was overlooked. And they were contacted even before the committed date arrived.

Ironically, the applied solutions didn't address the actual issue but they led to many more problems. And yeah, not even one single person took that pause. The concept of sticking around was overlooked. If only the heads of the respective departments had invested more time in sticking around for a while before addressing the imaginary issue, they would have identified the crux of the real problem.

13) No is difficult but yes is dangerous

Yes and no are two sides of the same coin.
But sometimes, the coin belongs to someone else.

A no or a yes are the simplest and most commonly used forms of verbal replies. This is our way of conveying that we have made up our mind. It's our way making our intentions clear. It is a stand that we take. Apart from giving enough clarity for a particular question, it denotes confidence. Saying a no or a yes is a big deal, personally and professionally both. It's like making that most crucial final decision. An entrepreneur makes numerous decisions in a day. Every single no or yes is a reflection of that decision. This could be a reply to an email he receives about a particular event invite. It could be a reply to a service provider that he doesn't think his company should continue with. It could be a meeting request from a client. It could be all sorts of crazy requests from his employees, from early going to late coming. And if he's handling a decently sized company, it could be questions from heads of various departments. It also could be an answer to an investor. It could be an answer to so many people he interacts with on a daily basis.

But whoever he deals with, and whatever the question he needs to reply to, it's an art to say a no or a yes. No is difficult but why yes? Isn't that supposed to be easy? Well, it sounds easy as it comes naturally to most of us. We don't really have to worry about disappointing someone. Also, saying no has been widely recognized as a common problem with most. So, a no is difficult. But a yes is dangerous. It has always been underplayed. It is dangerous because every repercussion of a yes leads straight to us. The ones on the other side of the table are mostly happy with our yes. If we make a decision, and wrongly say yes, we suffer the most. So, a yes is a dangerous answer to handle.

To say no is a difficult thing for some. These people could jump off a cliff, do the craziest adventure sport ever. But saying no is more like the end of everything for them. Their fear of saying no is so strong that they end up saying yes even when they wish to say no. In the end, the damage always shows up though. Saying no to those we've known for years is awkward. It becomes more of an obligation. And in business, obligations can't be ignored all the time. But because most of us are aware of how saying no is a difficult thing to do, we are more careful about it. We think, we analyze, and we make a call. But when it comes to saying a yes, we are naturally inclined towards it. We take that so-called easy route. The fear of saying no pushes us and we follow suit. We all know that saying no is difficult. But what we don't realize is that saying yes is dangerous. And that's where the problem is.

There are some really common situations where an entrepreneur has to choose between a no and a yes. For instance, this situation could be about taking up a business opportunity. We make pitches, or get enquiries. The difference is that when we make pitches, we're always closer to a yes. We already have the intent to work for the prospective client. However, there could be certain facts that we were unaware of. And that's when it's perfectly normal to reanalyse things before giving your ultimate decision. Making the first move and giving a pitch or a proposal does reflect one's interest in taking up the business. And it does imply that one has made up one's mind. So, a no at this stage could backfire too. It could show the company and the leader in a bad light. It could tarnish the image of the company. And that's exactly why it is a sensitive matter. It needs to be dealt with in a very calculated and mature fashion. There has to be a clear reasoning. The relationship, however, needs to be retained. You never know who moves where tomorrow, and you might have to face the same set of people on a different ground. And that's when the need will be yours more than anybody else's. But what could be the reason to say a no this far in the game? Well, maybe we were unaware of the fact that this prospective client is a bad paymaster. Incidentally, a bad paymaster is one of the worst things that can happen to a start-up, or even an established business, for that matter. The opportunity could be exciting and tempting both. But when you do understand that the client is a bad paymaster, it will always help to step away, and focus on the greater side of business. This category of clients is bad not just for start-ups. They've got the knack to push things beyond the accepted limits. So, one will always end up wasting time with regards to such prospects.

An incoming enquiry on the other hand is a different ball game altogether. This is when the person on the other end has high inclination towards working with your company. They've made the most coveted first move. The first move says a lot in business. It defines that the need is there. It assures that the conversion will happen. It conveys that there is some amount of dependency that exists. It can go out to prove that the person or company on the other side has done its share of research on the best in the business. And you're certainly one of the chosen few. But a yes or a no here is equally crucial. The limitations are much fewer though. With incoming enquiries, it's a yes that needs more thought than anything else. Those coming to you for business might have a clear purpose behind the whole thing. They must have identified you as the perfect fit to explore. Or worse, they must have identified you as the perfect fit to exploit. This is where a yes is more dangerous, for those who are uncomfortable with a no will face issues in this scenario as well. But one needs to do one's side of due diligence before allowing an enquiry of this nature to convert. That's because it would end up benefitting those on the other side of the table only.

Say no when your gut says so. We did explore the importance of instincts previously in the book. And it does tell us about how to get the best out of them. But instincts play a crucial role in decision-making too. Sometimes, we don't have clear reasons. But we still end up having clear answers. That's where our gut comes into play. It does come to our rescue in situations that could turn out to be completely in contrast to what is being promised. A prospect could seem great. You would have sealed the compensation, the plan, and the deliverables. But at every stage, something inside tells you that this is not the way to go. This could be just a misleading inner voice too. But even if it is misleading, more often than not, it does leave an imprint on you. And if it does, it's best to avoid the route. Well, some of the best routes to the most amazing destinations, when taken in doubt, will end up in a disaster only. So, if the seed of this doubt has been rooted deep inside us, it's better to stay away from such prospects. A no will be difficult as you're in the last leg of closing the deal, or you've already done that. The deal is tempting. And you do want to go ahead with it. It's more like a war within, a war between your mind and gut. Whoever wins, there are all chances that you could lose. So, a yes here could be the most dangerous thing to do.

Whether it's a no or a yes, it's good to know how and when to use each of these tools. Ignoring any one of these, just because you're comfortable with the other, can be more damaging than you think. At the end of the day, entrepreneurship is all about moving out of our comfort zone, outperforming ourselves, and building a brighter future for every single person who has been a part of our dream. It's about decision-making. It's about risk. It's about high stakes. It's about execution. It's about listening to your instincts, when everything else makes greater sense to the rest of the world. But most importantly, whether it's a difficult no or a dangerous yes, the ability to make the right decision at the right time will always come in handy. It will remain one of the most important aspects of entrepreneurship.

14) Law of reaction is passé

If every action had an equal and
opposite reaction,
there would have been no trace of
mankind any more.

As entrepreneurs, there's one thing that comes naturally to most of us—reaction. Well, it is good to react. In fact, it is important to react. But as an entrepreneur, one really needs to gauge the situation before one reacts. There are times when you need to react instantaneously. However, like any other rule, there are exceptions to this one too. When there's a crisis, any delay in your reaction can cost you that most crucial client, even worse, that most crucial employee. These things are very situational. But sometimes a situation like this can shatter many hearts, minds, and souls.

John Brown was the CEO of a digital media company in Connecticut. Apart from being a highly qualified digital marketer, he held a master's degree in business administration. He was the perfect blend of a leader with technical, analytical skills. He was good at operations too. But people management didn't come easily to him. He was short-tempered. And that always got in the way of him dealing with people in a more humane fashion. It was an area where he constantly faced issues. But there was one instance that changed his perception towards this subject. Moreover, he learnt how to handle people and certain situations better.

That morning, his reaction was neither instant nor well gauged. He had made up his mind that he would have to put his point across to all the employees, irrespective of how it would be perceived. He knew what he had to speak. In fact, he had it all written down with him. He believed in the fact that one of the fundamentals of preparing for an internal team meeting was to write down the points that had to be discussed. And he did just that. The difference, however, was that there was no room for discussion. It was one of the shortest one-sided meetings ever.

He walked out of the room and realized that in less than a couple of hours, his team was reduced by a good 35 per cent in size. It was like people were on a resignation spree. All of a sudden, people realized that the office was too far from their place, that their father had to undergo a surgery, that they were not being paid enough, so on and so forth. He didn't want to suspect whether their reasons were valid or not. But he wanted to understand what went wrong. His company hit an all-time low, in terms of employee morale and work environment; bad organizational health is how most books would describe this situation.

This episode was enough to break him from within. It has been with him since then. It took months for him to get out of this situation. People felt that he was just overreacting, and it was not a big deal. Companies do hit a rough patch of this sort. But what bothered him the most was the reason that led to this situation. Some key people of the company could sense that there was an issue that had to be addressed; that needed a quick and effective reaction. But he was still recuperating from that episode.

Soon, he realized that if he had to get things back to normal, it was imperative for him to fix himself first. Only then he could move ahead. He did try to walk down the path once again, in my mind, to figure out every single aspect. He revisited that situation quite a few times from a vantage point. But he felt that was not enough. He decided to get rid of assumptions and hear it from the horse's mouth.

The next step was to reconnect with those employees who quit that day. It was obvious that they were hurt; there was a lot of negativity that seeped in. He tried reaching out to his people. But there was a lot of resistance. He felt that one attempt would not fix this up. A lot of good was needed to kill the bad. Finally, it was perseverance personified. Once he managed to reconnect with his people, he spoke with no preconceived notions (a highly required and endorsed approach). He understood that it was all about the negativity that overshadowed everything else. The issue was the time of the day when they were spoken with (first thing in the morning) and the authoritative tone in which they were spoken with (one-sided). The problem was clear. Now was the time to clean up all the garbage that this caused.

This was not the time to analyze and work out solutions that would simply take care of the situation. This was the time to first clear the air, to have a healthy heart-to-heart conversation with no expected outcome. The idea was to make sure that the subject (our employee) gets undivided attention.

Well, we're mostly in a rush to move from negative to positive, quickly. What we don't realize is that to move from negative to positive, we need to get neutral first. That's exactly what was applied in this case. John didn't have any hidden agendas. The goal was clear—to get back to a normal relationship, like before. What happened next would shape up with time. So, that was his neutral point. This is when moving to positive seemed achievable, and things started falling into place.

This was an episode where a reaction destroyed, and later fixed up things. And that's only because it was not an equal and an opposite reaction. It was a high-intensity one initially, and a slow yet well-gauged one later!

15) Let's pass the fail test

*There's always a good idea in a pile of
stupid ones.
But the fear of failure stops us from
finding one.*

When there are so many inspiring subjects
and stories around us, we tend to get blinded by
success. We focus more on success and feel that
it is easily achievable. Yes, it is achievable. Easily
or not is another thing. But in the process of giving
undivided attention to success, we forget the fact
that it has a flip side. It is a side that not many can
cope with. It is a side that most of us shy away
from. It is a side that not most of us want to know
about. But it is a side that we all interact with. It
is a side that meets us all. In fact, there are few
successful entrepreneurs. So, we can't say that

every entrepreneur is successful. But it is pretty safe to say that every entrepreneur—running a start-up or a mammoth—would have seen failure at some stage in his journey, in some form or the other. So, technically, the importance of failure is a lot more in our lives. We all know that failure is the best teacher. And it is a stepping stone to success. But all that is so damn faded. We are all running after success at such a high speed that we forget to look at failure.

That's because no one wants to accept failure. Unfortunately, it is our fear of being written off. But the fear of failure is worse than failure itself. We, as entrepreneurs, begin to live under this constant pressure of showcasing success like never before. And that pressure takes away all the opportunities that we'd have if we'd embraced failure too. A closer look at failure will always help us look for a better route to reach success. The power of failure has always been reflected in the lives of some entrepreneurs who with unmatched perseverance marched towards their destination. It is these people who used failure as a fuel to bring about a positive change in the world of entrepreneurship.

But when we meet failure at the very beginning of our journey, it is heart-wrenching. It is difficult to put our energies together and move ahead. But that's the order of the day. It is something that every entrepreneur has to deal with.

Just talk about it openly

The funniest thing that we end up believing is that not talking about failure means we never failed. But contrary to that belief of ours, the more we talk about failure, the more we begin to get comfortable with it. The more we get comfortable with it, the more we drop the excessive baggage that success comes with. Talking openly about failure also helps us identify the drawbacks in our plans or execution. It brings us closer to those grey areas that we would have otherwise never noticed.

Accept the flaws it reflects

Acceptance, undoubtedly, is the first step towards improvement. By denying failure, we don't open up to the fact that there are flaws that have to be fixed. When we don't look at the flaws and accept them, all we end up doing is keep wondering, how did we even fail in the first place? It is the toughest analysis to make. But great entrepreneurs reached where they did by taking up this tough role, and executing it with great finesse. Perhaps, it is this ability of theirs that places them where they rightly belong— on a pedestal.

Immediate answer is not a mandate

It is certainly an art to handle failure. And not many are good at it. Sometimes, failure gets the better of us. When we come across failure, we place ourselves under so much pressure that we begin to look for some immediate answers. We don't even take a deep breath before we begin the hunt for answers. We seek immediate answers. Well, though it is great to get to the root of the issues as soon as possible, we need to understand that an instant answer is not a mandate. A sudden shift in situation takes time to cope with. No amount of hurry can make the process any simpler or more effective. The simplicity is in giving failure some time to settle down. That's when it becomes easier to gauge. That's when we can get to our answers better.

So what if it is a stigma?

Failure is not completely accepted in most societies. People tend to look down upon failure, primarily when that failure is someone else's. But the question to ask is, so what if failure is socially unacceptable? If we begin to look at it rather normally, we will be able to create a culture where people can embrace failure. It is only then innovation will happen at a much swifter speed. And an organization that openly innovates certainly sees some tremendous growth and breakthroughs.

Let it not weaken the core team

Failure is fluid in nature. It is easy for it to seep into the core team of an organization. It is much quicker in start-ups though. But even bigger organizations fall prey to this. When failure strikes, the leader of an organization has to set an example, and display strength that results in restored belief of his people. That's when the strength of a leader is tested. That's when he has to prove his mettle. He needs to absorb failure, and make sure it doesn't hit the morale of his key players. As long as we don't really work towards embracing it internally as well, it is going to put us in a difficult spot. In fact, embracing failure internally will work great in enhancing company culture—the one that focuses on innovation. More often than not, innovation comes with a price of failure. And when a team knows that the company is ready to pay that price, it will strike harder.

In business, we hit some. We miss some. And every entrepreneur is well aware of this fact. Nobody likes failure, for the sheer reason that it demonstrates inability or incompetency, of a leader and his team both. The reasons could be many. But it does create a roadblock in the way of an organization's growth. It raises a lot of eyebrows. It dilutes a lot of efforts and years of energy that every single person in the team must have put in. Perhaps that's why it is difficult to not just accept failure, but celebrate it too. The first step, however, is to accept it as part of the process of growth and experience. Once we do that, we'll be able to look at it straight in the eye. That's when we'll be prepared to take on any question that revolves around it. That's when we'll be able to look inside for answers that will help us improvise. And soon, we'll even be able to not just accept it but celebrate it too. Well, why not? At the end of the day, it does lead to organizations reaching some of the most challenging milestones. It does help organizations successfully pass the most coveted fail test.

16) When teamwork doesn't work

If we create a team, it becomes an asset.
If we don't, it becomes a liability.

One of the most commonly used terms in the entrepreneurial circles is *team*. The importance of a team doesn't stop at clients, who, with all due diligence, make sure they do business only with a company that's got the right team. The right team is equally important to the investors. In fact, the decision of most potential hires to accept respective job offers is also influenced by the existing team the organization's got. It is about the right combination that a leader needs to have. It is a structure that he needs to design. Only then this combination becomes truly lethal. The importance of creating this lethal combination increases as an organization evolves, right from being a start-up to transforming into a business giant. A good team doesn't stop at just being that; it comes to the rescue of a company in times of crisis. But sometimes, it becomes the sole reason for a crisis.

A team is all about teamwork. Whether it is athletes playing a sport on the field, chefs whipping up a meal in a restaurant, or musicians in a band playing at a concert, teamwork is the crux of every performance. As leaders, however, we tend to become complacent with our current team and its work. We get overly comfortable. We begin to think that this excess comfort will help us meet business objectives better. Unfortunately, that's mostly not the case. Excessive comfort in any business is way more harmful than no comfort!

Well, like everything else in the world, teamwork too has a flipside—groupism. Sounds familiar? It is obviously not a new term. It is a forgotten term. Teamwork defines the health of an organization. Groupism deteriorates it. There were times when companies feared only one thing—unions. For centuries, they ruled companies with an undertone of white-collar blackmail. Times have changed since then. Today, unions hardly exist. We don't really hear of them as much as we used to. And we believe that they have faded with time. That's not true though. Unions are not extinct. They are still found in companies of all sizes—start-ups, multinationals, et al. The truth is that, like companies, unions too have evolved. They are now identified as groups with a common cause. More often than not, this cause is unrealistic and injurious to a company's existence though.

In a start-up culture, or even a bigger organization, for that matter, nothing can be more powerful than the right team. It takes years for companies to get that perfect mix in a team. And when it does, it reflects on the work. Things begin to look better than ever before. But some people of a team can't handle success as well as the others. That's when they begin to assume all the praise and every round of applause belongs to them. It is when one or few members of a team begin to feel that they are bigger than the team. There is sporting history that has time and again shown that every legend was called that because he never felt he was bigger than the team or the sport. History has also been witness to the devastating end of some of the best teams in the world.

So, how does one make sure that the impact of this groupism is minimal on their company? Well, there's no sure-fire way of killing this impact but there are certainly precautions that one can take in the beginning of one's entrepreneurial journey.

Reduce dependency and hire more

Why is it even more important for start-ups to carefully pick every single member of the team? That's because in some cases this is a team of just three—one being the founder himself. That's how the beginning of most start-ups have been. Due to a very small team size, dependency becomes very high. A leader has to be on the constant lookout to reduce this dependency. This does not mean one has to fire their existing employees. It is not a war; it is just a way of making sure that the company is secure. And to do that, additional resource hiring is an option. It is certainly going to be an overhead. And for a start-up, one overhead means a lot. But at the cost of securing the company, having backups is not a huge cost. It is certainly worth it. Some call it contingency planning, and some call it organizational structure forecast. Whatever term you choose, keep the objective clear. Apart from hiring additional resource or resources and depending on your team size, business forecast, etc., cross-training also comes in handy.

Ban employee referral system

As strange as it may sound, more often than not, this one does help. The human resource department of big organizations makes efforts for employee rewards, recognition, engagement, fun at work, and a lot more. And none of that is bad. At the end of the day, a company is all about people. And it is about being fair to them. It is about being honest, transparent, sensitive, and empathetic with its employees. But the bigger cause here should be the company itself, the sole reason why this team is even together, the sole reason why a leader even exists. And a leader must do everything to protect this reason. Employee referral system is not as harmful to bigger organizations as it is to start-ups. The probability of seeding groupism is way higher when existing employees of a start-up begin to refer close friends. It somehow begins to fade the line between their personal and professional relations. And when one of them is underperforming, or is in line for the company to move ahead on its path, he becomes a bad influence on the others too, more so on the referred friend first. It is the perfect environment to nurture groupism and take shape into a mammoth calamity that can lead to the destruction of the start-up too.

Lead only if you really can

Groupism is not always the result of unrealistic approach or expectations of employees. It can also be a result of a leader shying away from his responsibilities. Being a leader doesn't make one right all the time. When a leader becomes unfair, groupism is inevitable. As leaders, it is our duty to work towards the interest of the company and the employees both. But sometimes greed, arrogance, overconfidence, or autocracy can seep into a leader. And that's when he becomes a bigger threat to the organization than anybody else. Groupism that arises from a leader who's not genuine will be more deep-rooted than you can possibility imagine. You can't be fair always. You can't keep everyone happy all the time. But most employees will value your genuine efforts in doing that. And that's when the result will not make that big a difference.

17) If perfection kills . . .

Perfection is like a medicine. When taken in excess,
it does more harm than good.

Achieve perfection. But don't expect perfection, especially when you delegate. That could be a highly debatable beginning. But in no way does it mean that high performance is disregarded. It just reiterates that every individual is different. Employees are human too. And sometimes their underperformance is involuntary. That's when leaders are expected to step in to understand that sometimes good enough is good enough.

Perfection is a term that's synonymous with most entrepreneurs. And in the early stages of a business, it comes in handy. For some, this eye for detail could be a point of differentiation too. But as business grows, it is humanly impossible for founders to continue doing what they used to. In the initial phase, they are used to doing things themselves. But to elevate their business, their contribution comes in the form of empowering their teams to do things. And this is where most entrepreneurs struggle. They look for people who work like them, who complete tasks like them. They begin to expect a reflection. What they tend to forget is the fact that even reflection is a flipped imagery of the actual subject!

However, in their run to achieve perfection, entrepreneurs ignore the following issues it begins to create:

- It leads to micromanagement, and that earns the ire of the employees. Employees thrive on confidence that higher-ups put in them. But if they're not directed right, they feel choked. In fact, it also puts entrepreneurs off track from their actual job of looking at the bigger picture of the organization.
- It tends to kill the morale of the employees, and puts a big break on areas like productivity, thereby substantially increasing expenses and creating a huge dent in profits. And that's certainly not a positive sign for any business.
- It increases attrition. With no milestones being achieved, people tend to lose interest in their jobs. And it is proven that

job satisfaction is mostly ranked above monetary benefits ·too. The flip side, however, is that sometimes it could also be demeaning to employees that they are wrongly perceived as underperformers, especially because perfection is subjective in nature. Hence, they begin to retaliate in an unusual or destructive way.

- It affects organizational health, as it becomes a bigger baggage than expected. That's because once the existing employees leave, three times more time, money, and effort are invested in hunting for, interviewing, recruiting, training, and retaining new employees.

This is when leaders have to shift focus from perfection. They need to realize that sometimes good enough is good enough. It is only when they loosen up a little, give room to subordinates, not make them self-conscious, and encourage an atmosphere where mistakes are reference points for improvement that there will be a positive change.

Though there are books that talk about the art of delegation and getting work done, the problem area mostly remains untouched. So, where exactly is the gap? Well, it is in understanding that achieving perfection is great. But expecting perfection, especially from everyone, can be harmful to an entrepreneur and an organization both.

When delegating work, unless the subordinate is highly exceptional, an entrepreneur has to be prepared for any shortfall that may show up. He will then slowly need to fill the gaps and help his subordinate cut down on the same, one after the other.

In a practical scenario, employees struggle in various areas. This could range from lack of clarity on a specific job to no proper training, from partial understanding of the subject to various other reservations. Hence, the job doesn't reach perfection. But perfection, contrary to popular belief, is not a destination; it is a journey. And when it begins to kill, remember that sometimes good enough is good enough!

18) The ride between delegation and deadline

*The smoothness of a drive doesn't just
depend on the road.
It depends on the driver too.*

These are two big words that most start-up
leaders would dread—*delegation* because they
would have spent most of their time in a DIY (do it
yourself) mode, and *deadline* because that is one
of the key metrics to ensure repeat business. But
most budding entrepreneurs face similar situations
where they are unable to rely on their team
member(s) and give away controls of a specific
task. And this is primarily because they feel that no
one would do it as well as them, forget better than
them. And in most cases this is a fact. But does

that mean companies don't grow? Start-ups don't transform into large organizations? Well, they do. But that's possible only when the leader begins to understand that with time, his role has changed. He needs to work harder, but differently. He is no longer in a DIY mode, exceptions excluded. And we shall talk about those exceptions a little later. This is when the leader is more of a catalyst. His victory is no longer about bagging that crucial piece of business, or executing that important task. His victory is when his team does it. He is more about exciting people, stimulating them.

Though all this sounds simple, an entrepreneur in this phase understands the difficulty of this transformation. If you are in this phase, you can be sure that it is not unique or uncommon. In fact, it is a great learning opportunity. It is a phase that will help you understand your strengths better. So far you were doing anything and everything. Now is when you'll need to narrow down that and create a job role for yourself and your partners, if applicable.

It is a fact that most leaders, even experienced ones, fear delegation. That's obviously because of thoughts like 'I do it the best' or 'No one cares for my brand as much' or 'I know he will screw up'. There are a zillion more reasons, rather excuses. Even if they do delegate, they're always on the lookout for that big flaw that reassures some of their many beliefs. But at the end of the day, one needs to understand that we can't be doing anything and everything all the time.

But people do dread delegation because of the stringent deadlines that most client requirements come with. The room for delay or error is minimal. The most difficult part for an entrepreneur falls between delegation and deadline. That's exactly where maximum drama builds up. That's where anxiety comes into play. That's where nervousness sees an all-time high. That's where the mind begins to go numb. But that's exactly where one's leadership qualities are of the utmost importance. The way you perceive this will mark the beginning of the first phase of your business transformation.

The irony, however, is that most parents would have taught us delegation way before we even decided to become an entrepreneur. Though a lot of youngsters are already sowing seeds of entrepreneurship in their mid-teens, there's a common set of advice that most middle-class parents give their kids, typically when they'd buy a new bike for their kid. Here's how it goes—'Always ride at a speed you can manage. Be careful on the road even if you are good. Always wear a helmet. Forecast traffic better—start early when you have to reach a destination at a specific time. Follow traffic rules.'

Well, that advice is not just for the road; it is for the road to success too—for riders and entrepreneurs both.

Ride at a speed you can manage

Let's replace the word *ride* with *grow*. Makes sense? When businesses begin to grow, sometimes leaders don't realize that excessive growth can backfire, same as excessive speed, more so when one can't handle it. Growth is great. It is a crucial metric to gauge the progress and market share of a business. But when a team is not prepared for this growth, organizations begin to tremble. And it is during these times that delegation becomes even more difficult. Hence, controlled growth is important to delegate better.

Be careful even if you are good

In a start-up scenario, delegation is of higher importance than in a sustained business that's been around for a while. As a leader, one could be the best when one's on the ground, doing things like anyone else in the team. But leadership and delegation is a different ball game altogether. One needs to understand that even if one is good, one needs to be prepared for the shortcomings of the others in the team. It is more like we could be the best drivers in the world, but when we are on the road, it is important to be prepared for the shortcomings/errors of that not-so-good driver.

Always wear a helmet

Well, most of us confuse protection with just being careful. Being careful, in terms of delegation, is more like creating room for any shortcomings of a teammate. However, protection would be more like a contingency plan, a plan B of sorts. This would help you escape from some unwanted bruises. This could range from buying extra time from the client to having a backup for the work that is to be shared. The previous heading talks about keeping some buffer so that you have enough time to fix problems. And that is something most people do comfortably. But this heading is more about being ready with a solution, in case of an emergency. And this is where delegation fails like never before.

Forecast better—start early

Starting early is more about what a leader can do to get better results from delegation. It is like 'early to bed, early to rise'. Or if you want to reach a destination at a specific time, leave early from home. And that's because you never know the kind of traffic and other issues that would come your way. As we move ahead with a start-up, transforming it into a successful company, we are compelled to forecast better. It is important to understand our current bandwidth. Most of us fail to accept the fact that we are short-staffed. And delegation in a short-staffed environment is mentally exhausting not just to the first-time executives or underperformers; it also begins to affect the senior lot.

Follow traffic rules

Well, like traffic rules, every organization has got a set of policies and rules. These vary from company to company, depending on the experience, expectations, goals, and skills of the leader, just the way we've got different traffic rules in different countries. But there are certain rules, sometimes unwritten, that are common across various companies. And to avoid accidents, it is significant to follow these rules. But as leaders and lawmakers, we tend to forget that we need to abide by them too. And when we break rules, it causes a bigger stir. It is like lawmakers turned lawbreakers. And these rules include analyzing skills of employees before a task is delegated to them, giving them time to move ahead on the learning curve, constructive feedback, the right amount of motivation, an approach that doesn't degrade them, willingness to embrace repeated mistakes, courage to channelize improvement, enough time to spend on review, and more.

19) Ignorance is bliss
. . . for managers

Managers should be like dolphins;
they should sleep with one eye open.

Ever wondered why the word *patience* gets a lot of importance in any leader's dictionary? One of the reasons is that patience is a great teacher. It teaches you a lot of things, if you choose to learn. Just being patient doesn't help. That's the reason why some leaders, despite being patient, are not very successful. That's because patience is more like the pause that we discussed in one of the previous chapters. As much as we specify the importance of that pause, what also can't be denied is how you choose to use it. If you use it judiciously, it adds a lot of value to all the efforts that you've put in. On the flip side, if you take a pause only to make sure that you don't react in a destructive way, it wouldn't be of much help. At work, we're strategizing, we're developing people, we're building a brand; wrestling is a different ball game altogether. But if that's your idea of leadership, join an underground fight club!

Now that you do understand the importance of a pause, it is important you also focus on how this pause, a symbol of patience, can be truly effective.

Paul Hickman, an MBA graduate, joined his first job in a leading multibillion-dollar company as a management trainee. This was in the early '80s, when a job in one of these companies was placed pretty high on a pedestal. He was too excited about the fact that this was where he'd get maximum exposure. He was also looking forward to put into practice all the knowledge he had gained during his course. He was a lot like any other MBA graduate who had passed recently. But he had the gift of patience. He used to come across as a bit indifferent to people and situations. But people couldn't understand that he was a sharp guy. He was constantly thinking. When he seemed to be completely disconnected from the world around him, he was actually the most connected. This quality of Paul was not really received as a good quality though. But the business head of his process was pretty much aware of this. In fact, he was the one who took Paul on board.

As managers (or even if you are a trainee), you'd soon fall into a pit full of people. Paul's manager was struggling to meet the SLA (service level agreement). SLA is an agreement that a company signs with a client, and this is where you spell out the deliverables. It is a document that is based completely on the word *commitment*. Failing to meet these deliverables can have a very negative impact on the business. Paul was thrilled to have faced an issue like this in the early days of his career. When his manager was trying to make both ends meet by leaving no stone unturned, Paul was quiet. In fact, he was almost frozen. But deep down inside, he was on the job to fix this situation. As negative a word as it might sound, ignorance is of high importance in leadership, especially when you are handling a team. Paul would see the repeated attempts that his manager would make to correct his team. It was like his manager was more of a watchdog, who was always on the hunt for the crooks. Every time someone made a mistake or drifted away from the process, his manager would step in and correct it himself. Sometimes he would not really correct it. But he would certainly point out the issue. Paul's manager continued to point out every single mistake that his people would commit.

But this attitude of his never helped him fix these issues. One day, Paul decided to step in and share his thoughts with the manager in a one-to-one discussion. The first question that Paul asked his manager was if he'd seen any change in the behaviour of his team in the last few years.

The manager said, 'No. That's how these guys are. I don't think they will ever improve.' Paul was expecting an answer like this. He then said, 'I know I am just a trainee at the moment. But if you allow me to share my point of view without any inhibitions, it would be great.' The manager was slightly surprised as Paul was pretty new to the system. But he wanted to know what was going on in Paul's head. So he asked him to move ahead. Paul then said, 'There's only one reason why the team has not improved. And that reason is you.' His manager was a bit uncomfortable with the remark that Paul made. He wanted to stop the conversation right there. But then he felt that he had come this far. And it was best that he at least ask Paul to justify that statement of his. And he did just that. Paul replied, saying, 'If you always keep checking the employees for such minute details, they will feel that you are micromanaging them. And once they begin to feel that, they will lose their sole purpose of the job. They will feel less responsible, thinking that you are anyway checking every single bit.' The manager felt that Paul did make sense. But he wanted to know more. He asked Paul to continue. Paul added, 'Sometimes it's best to ignore a few mistakes. And if you really think they should be addressed, you need to look for the right time to talk about them. Most importantly, try to blend them with constructive feedback. This would clearly help you cite an area of improvement, and get some results. The best practice, however, is to solve these issues, one at a time.'

The manager was stunned by the advice Paul had given him. He knew that he was blinded with day-to-day activities, and the zoomed-out perspective of Paul was the much-needed break. He was always in a rush to execute but never spent time in observing the core issues and looking for a solution. But after that discussion with Paul, he tried working in sync with his advice. It, however, took him a long time to break away from the impression that he had created on his team. He had to work harder to get rid of their preconceived notions about him. He had to start afresh. But slowly, he began to see some results. And that encouraged him to move ahead in the direction shown by Paul.

So that's how Paul was able to make a positive difference. For this, he just had to stay calm, zoom out, and observe. It's a myth that one needs to always be quick to execute. In reality, sometimes one has to slow down and watch. Similarly, there's another myth that does the rounds—you can learn about business and leadership only from books that cover these subjects, or mentors who must have spent their life running an unsuccessful business but love to preach during the last innings of their life. The fact is that these lessons can be learnt from everyday life. The people you deal with, the places you visit, and the episodes you come across, scream their heart out to bring these lessons closer to you. But all you have to do is observe what is important, and ignore the junk—especially if you are a manager.

20) Vacuum between what's said and understood

If communication didn't need common sense,
even donkeys would communicate as well as dogs.

Communication, they say, can break all barriers. It is simple but undoubtedly the most misused and underplayed word in an organization. It is not just important in the written form. Verbal communication is equally important. Whether it is a multibillion-dollar company or a mere start-up, the vacuum of communication prevails everywhere.

Big organizations feel that they are far away from communicating openly and clearly with those who are at the bottom of the ladder, the ones who actually execute. That's because either these companies feel that the gap is too huge to fill or they are plainly complacent. Then there are additional reasons like politics, misconception, expectations, and human emotions that form the rest of the story. Nevertheless, this is an area that has also got dedicated teams in many companies, for instance, the HR department that communicates with employees. But those are all frills. These so-called teams rarely connect with the people in a more humane way, the way it should be done. There are processes and protocols that these teams have to follow. But the difficult part is that when we deal with people, sometimes, structures and rules have to take a back seat.

Contrary to the popular belief, communication is way more difficult in start-ups, despite the fact that it is a small set of people who work closely. That's because the fewer the people, the higher the expectations. And the possibility of expectations not being met is high too. The higher the chance of them not being met, the sooner things would spread. If not addressed on time, this gap gets bigger by the day.

One such instance happened in a medium-sized software company called Matrix Lyne Technologies. This company used to render support to quite a few bigger giants in the market. This time they were approached by one of the biggest names in the market. They had to shortlist and send six employees to different client locations, in multiple cities in the country. The crisis was big and the team had to be on their toes to fix this.

As the team comprised six members at different locations, it became even more difficult for them to communicate clearly. Obviously, they had the luxury of videoconferencing. But communication is all about consistency. You can't be great one day and go dull the other. You'll always need to keep up with this challenge. Having been working on the same project, they needed to be on the same page.

Incidentally, this project was assigned to Robert Johnson aka Rob (that's how he'd preferred to be addressed). A tall and fair chap with a strong build and a thick pair of reading glasses that he would occasionally hang from his neck, Rob had enormous experience in his domain of coding. He had a very interesting career graph too. Interesting because he'd rejected a promotion four times in a span of around eleven years. The reason was that Rob loved to do the real job. In his opinion, the real job was what people at the bottom of the pyramid did: coding, in his case. He didn't take up a promotion, as any next post would put him straight into a managerial role. And he would have to stay away from the real job.

This project was crucial for Matrix Technologies. So, the senior management decided that this team would first be trained to understand what the primary issues were, and what could be the possible solutions. So, before this team of six departed, they went through an exhaustive three-day training program with Rob.

On the very first day of training, Rob moved straight to the point. He didn't focus on things like icebreaking, rapport building, or skill analysis. He jumped to the topic that was the main bone of contention. He didn't even focus on some overview or history, to make sure that all his trainees were on the same page. Then he made his first big mistake: he assumed that the trainees were aware of the basic issues that they had to deal with. Though his trainees were the best that the company could pick, the vacuum was evident. But this time around, the vacuum was not skill related; it was awareness related. Unfortunately, one of Rob's trainees, Benny D'Cruz, was unaware of a few details on the project. He had his own share of reasons; before Benny moved his focus to this project, he was working on something else. So, it was obvious for him to be a little less informed than the others. Benny tried catching up. But Rob demanded perfection, every single time, right from the very first time, and would not settle for anything less. This put Benny in a bigger fix. He knew he was on an uphill task. What he did not know was the fact that this uphill task had many hurdles. Benny screwed up something terribly on the first day of the training. And Rob was clear that this screw-up was unacceptable. So, he decided to share his unhappiness with Benny in a very crude way. This stern behaviour of Rob continued through the first day. And Benny lost track of the areas that he had to work on. Rob would not accommodate any slip-up. Also, because of this rift between Rob and Benny, others in the team began to doubt themselves. Not their fault—the human brain works in multiple dimensions as we watch external episodes very closely, especially when we can relate to any of these episodes.

Meanwhile, because of the attitude that Rob displayed, Benny was not very comfortable asking him questions to get more clarity on the subject. The reason was simple; Rob never displayed his openness for questions or concerns that the team would have. He came across as someone who was unapproachable. People in the team would talk to him in a very neutral way. But when it came to work, they preferred to maintain distance from him.

On the other hand, Rob thought that things were fine and Benny was the only person in the team who lacked the skills to take this project ahead. This prejudiced opinion that he had formed about Benny was the big spoiler. No efforts could solve this biased approach. The other notion was that it was enough to give clear explanation to his subordinates. Despite repeated explanation on the same subject, Benny could not finish a given task in the right way, without a slip-up. But post-explanation, Rob would always ask Benny if he understood what was explained. And Benny nodded his head positively, every single time.

Well, by then, it was too late for Benny to raise a question or a doubt. That's because Rob, during his very first interaction, had closed all doors of communication surrounding questions, doubts, help, and other related subjects. The irony was that initially he never made efforts to ask Benny what was his understanding of the subject, and moved ahead swiftly only on the basis of his assumptions. By now, it was absolutely unrealistic to expect that Benny would actually want to raise a concern. Rob felt that the best thing he could do was to give many instructions to Benny that would help him complete a specific task, which was true. What Rob didn't gauge, however, was how much Benny actually did understand of these instructions!

Well, firstly, giving instructions is not really the best way to get your people to work. That's because this way you break them down to mere followers who are not accustomed to using their own brain; they end up being a clone of you. And they stop functioning the moment they face a roadblock. But when you are training someone, instructions are to be given in the form of knowledge sharing. Hence, at times, it is a good thing to give clear instructions to people. But you need to understand that your clarity in no way reflects the clarity that the person on the other side of the table would have. The first rule of communication is to make sure that you are on the same page as the other person. That's how the journey would be more fruitful. Most of us assume that we are on the same page, partly because we expect the others to have some basic knowledge about various subjects and partly because we misjudge their basic understanding of a subject, though our judgment, at times, is a result of how others portray themselves. But that's not reason enough to make a wrong beginning to a discussion. It is our responsibility, as communication initiators, that we gauge how much the other person understands and how aware he is of the subject that we're dealing with.

This also takes us back to one of our previous subjects—stick around. The pause that we discussed previously need not necessarily reflect in just waiting or being strong when a problem strikes; it also holds good for taking a deep breath to identify the right time to do the right thing. This is something that Rob overlooked. He didn't feel the need to stick around before he could write off Benny. In the very first instance, his subconscious mind had decided that Benny was a clear misfit. This single thought of his sabotaged Benny's morale, and from being an average performer due to lack of awareness on the subject, Benny dropped to being a poor performer.

Training is a subject that relies heavily on communication. But the biggest misconception is that those who are good at what they do can easily teach others. The most successful teachers, however, are not those were good at their subject matter; they are the ones who had the required communication skills. Though this midsized company was being run by people who were experienced and qualified, they were terribly ignorant of the fact that a team should be led by a people's person who knows the importance of clear and open communication. He need not necessarily be a technical expert. And Rob was a clear misfit in that zone.

When we have to train people on a given subject, we need to get into their shoes, be more empathetic and encouraging while communicating. This is one area where technical skills would not help much. Communication is all about being human and addressing any vacuum. When we ignore doing that, in the long run, the human aspect is completely lost.

21) Let business meet fun, technically speaking

An entrepreneur should be like a versatile actor.
He should be good at comedy, drama, and romance.

Most of us think of a start-up as a home ground to all the technical knowledge we have acquired over time. When we have a great product or a service that's designed and developed by us, a start-up is born. When we acquire a certain skill that has the potential to drive the market, a start-up is born. We've heard a lot of stories about how the idea needs to be big, and everything else falls in place. Well, inspiration is good to help you move ahead in times of crisis. But a blinded inspiration is as harmful as no inspiration. You can't be feeling great about your start-up all the time. It is a misconception that as long as your subject matter is in place, you are good to roll. If subject matter alone could drive businesses, companies would not have business development profiles, actors would not have managers, and so on. To be able to create and sell is a rarity. Not many people can do that effectively. That's also one of the reasons why founders look for co-founders. Unfortunately, we run miles away from this fact. In the process, we end up failing in our ventures. Obviously, this is not the only reason why businesses sink. But it is one of the primary ones.

It was 1.30 p.m. A fairly young team of a newly formed company is all excited about their first pitch meeting. The meeting was fixed by one of the founders of the company—Roger, 29, known as Rog to most. He's a hard-core technology guy. He understands codes and technology like nobody's business. Coming from a humble background, Rog does understand the complex nuances of providing low-cost yet effective solutions to his clients. He believes that the price can be low or high. But the value should always be optimum.

The other founder was a numbers guy—Will, 31. He'd spent a considerable amount of his career playing with numbers. He was the guy who was responsible for making sure that the company is cash-flow positive. Will feels that at the end of the day, a business is as good as its balance sheet. And everything else, including technology, processes, clients, and portfolio, is secondary. Apart from

Rog and Will, the company had another founder who joined a little later—Dan, the operations guy. Well, that was his role. But he had a lot more stuff up his sleeve. He knew less about technology and cared little about numbers. His only focus was on driving their brand ahead. And he understood that a good combination of technology and numbers was not enough.

Here are three individuals who belong to three different schools of thought yet share one common goal—business. Rog had an advantage over the others; he knew the client since his very first job as a recruitment executive. And he kept in touch with the client ever since. So, the client was well acquainted and comfortable with Rog.

It was 2 p.m. now. They just reached the client's office. They were all set to enter the cabin. Everything seemed moving with the flow. The energy was pretty positive though it was clouded with a bit of nervousness. But that seemed okay for the flow. The client walked in. Initial greetings were exchanged. And all four of them sat down to take the meeting ahead. The client already had a heads-up about the agenda of the meeting and the new company that these founders launched. As Rog knew the client, he was leading the meeting. Quite predictably, Rog began talking and discussing technology with the client. The client was responding too. But he didn't seem to be taking a lot of interest in the conversation. His interest levels were dropping. And it became quite evident. Rog was so engrossed in the conversation and technology that it came across as a boring exam that he was putting the client through.

Sensing this somewhere in between, Dan pitched in. He changed the topic to something more generic, more neutral. And the client was immediately impressed with him. Dan had a way with words. He knew what to talk about, when to talk. He knew exactly how to impress and influence people on the other side of the table. And just one sentence was enough for the client to shift all his focus towards Dan. They began talking like long-lost friends. Surprisingly, they didn't speak a word about technology, or numbers, for that matter. The conversation was more generic. It was about common interests. Yes, that's a great way to establish an initial rapport with strangers. It could be a client or even a colleague; commonalities mostly work.

The meeting lasted long, and went well. Both parties agreed to work together. And a date was fixed to meet again to complete the formalities. Until here, technology was always in the back seat. Accompanying it was numbers. The client seemed pretty convinced about the people he was signing up with. He didn't have any major hassles with the numbers too. And was ready to sit across the table in the next meeting, and work on something mutually comfortable. And suddenly, the first project was more of a reality for this new company.

A start-up is a lot more than just a great product or a service. At the end of the day, it has to sell. And to sell, it has to make alliances. For this, it is very important for people behind to be able to strike up a conversation. That's because conversations lead to meetings, meetings lead to projects, and projects lead to alliances. Most of us, either with experience or naturally, end up being masters of the game. Well, there are some who are unable to cope, and they filter out with time. But the ones who stay in the game grab this well. But there's a big link that goes missing here. And that link categorically describes the whole idea behind why only technical skills would not suffice to drive businesses. The link is the extension of this chain. It is because of this missing link we don't really give as much importance to this aspect. So what's this missing link? We all know that conversations lead to meetings, meetings lead to projects, and projects lead to alliances. The missing link here is that alliances lead to conversations again; it then becomes a cycle that is imperative for good health of an organization.

22) Science behind the art of diversifying

Diversification is not rocket science.
But it's a science.

Every business is unique. And so should be the way to run it. Entrepreneurs are mostly thrilled about their ideas, their start-ups. It is what they eat, breathe, drink, and sleep. It is this zeal that helps them through the initial phases of their business. The ones who lack the zeal filter out midway. The rest begin to sail. And amongst the ones who sail, some turn out to be the giants of tomorrow. But every giant has a few things in common with others. Of course, there's no sure-fire formula to transform a start-up or a medium-sized business into a giant. But if we do study these giants closely, we'll see some similarities between them. And one of the top three similarities is diversification. Most of these companies started off with limited offerings in terms of categories. Soon they scaled to reach out to more customers. Most of them began to cover bigger geographical territories, and increase their customer base. But after a point, they could see that they were getting closer to saturation. And that's when they decided to diversify in terms of their offering. The obvious route for most of these was to diversify into related segments, and slowly diversify into segments that are way beyond their comfort zone.

Amazon, for example, started off as a virtual bookstore. The number of books that were available on Amazon was increasing by the day. The initial vision of the company was also synonymous with their name—Amazon. They wanted to be a dense collection of almost every possible book on the planet, just like the Amazon rainforest has a dense collection of species. Once the company felt that they had virtually every book available on their website and they were reaching out to as many customers as possible, they began to diversify. And this diversification was into related segment categories like CDs, software, etc. They added one category after the other. After adding most of the related categories, they added categories that were away from what they were known for. And slowly these new categories became the area of focus for them. Next, the new virgin categories were added swiftly, making Amazon the place for everything.

Today, they don't just operate in various countries across the globe. They also offer categories so diverse that there's hardly a thing one will not find on Amazon.

But you are not Amazon. You'd want to be one? Great. But you are not one today. So, do work your way up. But take it slow. Be careful about diversifying. Understand that diversification is a combination of art and science both. Don't diversify because you have heard of successful stories of start-ups diversifying and transforming into giants. Well, most of us are aware of some interesting stories about how these giants diversified and transformed into the companies that they are today. But there are also some less-known stories of how some great companies lost the game in bid to diversify.

Procter & Gamble's detergent Tide is an interesting example. The company was researching into detergents for a decade but was unsuccessful in creating the first synthetic non-soap detergent. The project was termed as Project X. In the year 1945, the work on creating this synthetic detergent was in full swing. Project X quickly moved from a backchannel research oddity to the forefront of P&G's product development. Tide was chosen as the name, though no one can recall why. In 1946, P&G began product testing in six cities. The marketers and branders quickly swung into action. Tide was an instant marketing success, selling out in markets all over the country as quickly as P&G could make it. Tide quickly boosted Procter & Gamble's share of the laundry market. By the early 1950s, Tide had captured more than 30 per cent share of the laundry market, and it has been the number one selling laundry detergent every year since. In 1970, Tide contributed over 50 per cent of all profits for P&G, despite the fact that the company comprised over sixty brands.

But soon Tide introduced certain variants in the detergent segment. They wanted to connect with more households. These variants were the perfect example of diversifying in the same category. But instead of boosting their sales, this strategy backfired. The number of variants began confusing people. They were not sure if they had to pick up the Tide Jasmine variant or the Tide Plus variant. This created a sense of confusion and doubts in the minds of the target audience. Hence, people began exploring more options. Their exploration moved them to try other brands of detergents. That's how soon a good percentage of their customer base shifted to other new brands, thereby diluting their market share. Perhaps, this is one of the best examples of how diversifying is a combination of art and science both.

While diversifying, it is not just the category or geographical location that matters. Perfect timing, the right market analysis, competitive study, clear forecast, predicted numbers, and a customer need are some of the factors that matter the most. Along with all this, the positioning of a diversified service or product needs to be conveyed clearly to the end customer. And that's because it is this positioning that will make sure that the end customer is not confused and will be able to make the right call in a jiffy. It is not just the bigger organizations that fall prey to this double-edged sword. Start-ups struggle equally. In fact, some start-ups end up moving away from their core objective, thereby creating an unclear image of what they truly excel at. Of course, clients love one-stop solutions. But they are never loved at the cost of the right quality. Hence, diversification should be given enough time by start-ups. An initial approach of a specialist works great for start-ups and gives them the much-desired visibility. Once they achieve a certain standing and get a foothold in the market, they can slowly plan for diversification. But when this process is not done in a strategic manner, it backfires and destroys what takes decades to build—the brand!

23) Celebrate milestones but place them differently

A milestone doesn't define a journey.
It's the journey that defines a milestone.

Milestone is synonymous with words like *business*, *organizations*, and *entrepreneurs*. It is what litre is to a liquid—a measure. It is like any degree or credential that you'd have, more of a brand value of an organization and an individual both. We all know the dictionary meaning of the word *milestone*. In fact, this word is overtly used in a zillion places like presentations, annual meetings, client reviews, appraisals, etc. We hear this word so often that it almost puts us to sleep.

Celebrating milestones is certainly one of the best things an organization and a leader can do. It peps up the environment, boosts the productivity of its people, and helps the organization climb up the ladder. But in this quantitative world, where every conversation has to lead to a visible gain, every meeting has to lead to a materialistic conclusion, every penny has to lead to a negotiation, we tend to place our milestones with an approach that is too narrow, and sometimes hollow; we place them where the results are.

An organization is never about a single person. As much as you call yourself the leader who has done it all, it is always about a set of people, despite the fact that you've been responsible for bringing these people on board. Entrepreneurs tend to get way too aggressive while placing their milestones. At times, they are so aggressive that they tend to ignore any other person who's associated with this milestone. The situation then looks something like this—a leader who's seeing a milestone clearly, has conveyed it to his team as clearly, is moving at a fast pace towards it and is also pushing his team with the same force. His team, however, just pretends to be moving with as much zeal. And what comes next is a reality check. Post a half-yearly review, the leader along with his team is nowhere closer to the milestone.

Well, the reason was that the team was never in consensus with the leader. They felt that the milestone he set was too unrealistic. Now, you may argue that you'll never be able to set a milestone that would be accepted by every single person of your core team. This is possibly a realistic and a common scenario too. But have you ever heard of the word *majority*?

Exactly! When majority of your core team decides to agree with your milestone(s), the probability of you, as a company, achieving it is way higher. At least this way, you know that more than 50 per cent of your team is with you. In fact, you can get them to set the milestones for themselves. This way, they'd be taking more ownership of reaching these milestones too.

This is an unorthodox way of placing milestones. The only difference is the fact that the probability of achieving these milestones is a bit higher. The flip side, however, is that your core team might not necessarily be as aggressive as you are. Hence, it might work out milestones that are less aggressive. But they'd certainly be more achievable. Here, the choice is yours; you can either set milestones that look great on paper but might not necessarily sound realistic and achievable to your team, or you can let your core team set simpler but highly achievable milestones.

In our day-to-day rush to meet business challenges and work towards innovation, we tend to forget that milestones can be placed differently. In business terms, a milestone is perceived as a destination. Very few leaders feel it is a journey. But one of the most effective placements of a milestone is somewhere in between.

To evaluate the effectiveness of this strategy of placing a milestone, an art director of an advertising company invited a few creative writers. These writers were divided into two teams—Team A and Team B. Both teams were given a brief to work on a launch campaign for one of its clients. This was the launch of a new energy drink—Octane. The client wanted to position their drink in the premium segment. They were well aware of the existing market leader in this segment. Because of smaller marketing budgets, they wanted something that was not just a strong launch campaign, but would also help them place their product in the premium segment. The writers put on their thinking caps, and began to pen some interesting ideas. After a long brainstorming session, both teams realized that they had to create an aspirational value for the brand. They also decided to focus on their target audience who'd in turn become brand loyalists. The teams then started working independently.

One of the creative communication ideas by Team A was to create an in-your-face ad concept to take the market leader head-on. The headline for this concept was 'Wings are for birds. Real men fly with Octane!'

Team B, on the other hand, worked on a concept that was subtle but equally strong. The headline for their concept was 'Octane—packed with NEWclear energy.'

Both the concepts were shared with the client. The creative director of the advertising company chose to reward one of the teams (Team A) the moment the concept was shared with him. However, he was not too convinced about the concept that Team B shared. He knew it was great too but he decided to wait until he heard from the client.

After a few days, the client got back to him, saying that they liked the concept by Team B better. In fact, they shared a very valid reason for the same. They felt that though the first concept was strong, it clearly divided their audience and boiled their product down to only-for-men.

The creative director then realized that he had misjudged the client, and the idea that was shared by Team B. He, later, decided to call Team B and reward them too. By now, both the teams were rewarded. The only difference was the timing. Though the concept shared by Team B was finally approved by the client and they were rewarded by the creative director, they didn't really like two things about him—he rewarded them only after the client approved their concept and the fact that he rewarded Team A way before he heard from the client. There was clear discrimination and he came across as biased. However, what didn't really work for him was the timing.

The idea of placing milestones differently is more about understanding the fact that a milestone is not a destination, it is not even a journey; it is in between! Well, in business terms, the journey in this case was the process that involved the teams working on ideas. And the destination was the client approving these ideas. But only if we choose to place our milestone when we are closer to the destination and where we have put in all our efforts, it would work wonders for an organization and its people. We can choose to, without discrimination, reward our people and celebrate the mere fact that the best efforts were put in. This should be an unbiased approach, irrespective of the final outcome (client's approval, in this case). This might not necessarily guarantee the project to you. But this will certainly let your people know that you value their efforts purely as they are, without being biased or influenced by any external factors.

The milestone is best placed where all the efforts are put in—just before the destination is reached.

24) Shift goals to goal the shifts

Despite the right technique, if you're unable to hit the bull's eye, move the target, and try again.

Strange? It isn't, actually. All you need to do is take a closer look at things, and you'll know why a shift in goal is the way to go. It is a fast-paced world. Things evolve even before we settle down with a goal. Every second, innovation shines upon us a sparkling new ray. An idea is no longer just our property. By the time we know that we're closer to a blueprint of an idea, it is already out in the open. All it ends up being is a new setback for us. There's nothing else that's new about the idea. But that doesn't mean that people today meet fewer goals than before. But yes, the way we move ahead towards a vision can be re-looked at. A static vision and a static goal is a thing of the past. It is perfectly okay to shift your goals a little, and readjust them to align with various influential factors like market conditions, competition, customer response, and many more. The turnaround time for a reaction today has boiled down to split seconds. So, a static goal could end up doing more harm than good.

Determination, conviction, and belief are good as long as you know that you are moving ahead on the right path. And daylight is at least slightly visible from where you stand. But it is also important for a business owner or a leader to sense when to make the right shift in the goal. It could purely be based on instincts too. The idea, however, is to constantly evaluate and improvise a certain goal. It is not necessary that this shift in goal can be done only when you are going great as a business. In fact, it is as valid to do this when things hit an all-time low too. The goal can be readjusted and moved as long as the vision is clear. Remember that even if the situation is perfect to have a sturdy goal, and all influential factors point towards having one, an erratic vision or a weak leader could be a big spoiler. There's no point in having a sturdy goal when your vision is unclear.

There have been innumerous examples in the past that reiterate the fact that a goal evaluation is sometimes the best thing to do. In fact, companies have done that in an effective manner too. A leader, however, risks the chance of coming across as indecisive or fickle minded.

But that should be a fair price to pay as long as one has got enough reasoning behind that crucial shift in goal. It should be a fair price to pay, as long as there is enough faith that his core team puts in him. It should be a fair price to pay, as long as he can make that big move towards a brighter tomorrow for the company and his people both. It should be a fair price to pay, as long as he can make sure his product or service adds more value to his customers.

These shifts, however, are not as easy as they might sound. Well, that's because it is not just about the leader here; it is also about a whole bunch of people who are following him. A goal shift is not a solution to every issue. But when market conditions demand, it could be a very sensible thing to do. Things like introducing new product categories, repositioning of a brand, and diversification into related verticals are all results of re-evaluated goals. In fact, there have been examples of companies that have completely moved away from their core business, the one that they started their journey with. Somewhere down the line, they decided to take the plunge and move towards a radically different market. And that move proved to be successful for them. They managed to get the recognition and market share they were vying for.

A goal shift is a part of entrepreneurship today. It is a crucial part of company strategy. It need not necessarily mean plan B. But it's somewhere close. It is about a company beefing up against volatile markets. It is about a leader taking all the necessary care to strike gold. It is about a bunch of people with an aggression to make a vision a reality. It is not a tell-all autobiography. It is a gamble that one plays. So, using the right cards at the right time is what matters the most. However, sometimes it is okay to bluff. That's when, more than timing and the cards, it is the confidence that becomes paramount in importance. So, whenever a leader decides to share his intent with the team, what matters is how much conviction he reflects. What also matters is how one can make this conviction infectious. If the leader needs more time to put things together, and get that much required confidence, it is okay for him to guide the ship towards new territories without being so very explicit to his team. The team can be informed when he understands that he's closer to a new destination—a more positive one.

But what if this goal shift backfires? Like everything else in the world, a goal shift has got a flip side too. And when things are not perfectly timed and one is not swift enough to move towards a goal that's in the process of shifting, it is bound to hit back. And that's exactly what makes it even more difficult. That's exactly why it needs a lot more focus. That's exactly why a leader and his core team need to constantly keep evaluating every move they make towards this shift. It is all being done at a decent speed. So, there isn't any time for a leader to sit back and mull over this. All the action is happening in a simultaneous fashion. And one needs to keep tabs on various aspects. This could be a tough spot to be in. But it can turn out to be more productive than years of work. So, it is a fair deal. But if it does backfire, one needs to make sure it is turned in a direction where damage is the least. A leader needs to be on his toes while making this decision. He will not have the time to take that most important pause before making a final call. He'll need to do all this when things are moving at a great speed. He will need to be a step ahead in the game. Perhaps that's exactly why not everyone can be a great leader. But every single person can certainly contribute towards a company trying to get a strong foothold while making this much-needed goal shift. And when we effectively work towards a shift in goals, that shift becomes our very goal.

25) Luck, hard work, and everything in between

Luck defines perception.
Hard work defines perseverance.

When we talk about entrepreneurs, businesses, dreams, plans and goals, how can we leave the age-old debate behind? It's a debate that tries to decode if successful people are hard-working or plain lucky. Over the years, we have seen a lot of legends. We've heard them, read about them, watched them, and analyzed every single move of theirs. Some of us end up thinking that successful people are lucky to have a specific skill-set. With technological and other advancements around the world today, people also think that these successful people were born at the right time. Which also means that they were lucky to be born in an era when competition was not fierce. When innovation was not happening at a rate that it is happening today. When there were too many gaps all round. When there were a lot of opportunities to solve a number of problems that a consumer was facing. Well, it could be assumed to be an era when it was comparatively easy to make it big. That's what some of us think, don't we? Especially when the leader in us has just begun his journey, and is trying to get his first breakthrough. It could be a moment that will give him the much-needed boost—this could be the first contract or the first crucial project. But it's that phase when we're trying to get a foothold. To the world it may seem easy. But entrepreneurship is in no way easy. It's a tedious process. It drains us. And if you think you're the unfortunate one to face tonnes of issues, you can rest assured that you're not the only one to go through moments like these. It's been a part of every entrepreneur's life, including the legends that we look up to. We all see the success. It's easy to identify with. It's always in the limelight. But what we don't see is years of struggle behind that success. What we don't see is the perseverance, the belief that these legends had during their share of testing times. The idea of discussing this subject is not to take a philosophical or a preachy route. But it's more about the fact that entrepreneurship is difficult. It's not everyone's cup of tea. It's not just for the lucky ones. It's actually for the hard-working ones. We've read a lot about the importance of hard work, and how it has been a differentiating factor between the successful and the unsuccessful. But when the time comes, we forget that basic yet most important lesson of our life—there is no substitute for hard work.

As an entrepreneur, you'll have to put in countless hours into moving towards your goal. You'll have to make those sacrifices. When the whole world is celebrating and having a good time, you'll have to keep moving towards your mission. When the world is sleeping, you'll have to stay up to plan your next move. Remember that it's not abnormal. It's a ground rule, more of an unwritten one. Entrepreneurship is highly demanding. And that's exactly why people fail to connect with it. Ironically, if entrepreneurship were really that easy, every single person around us would be an entrepreneur today, and a successful one at that. Entrepreneurship is a fire, an addiction to make things happen. It's a belief. It is the will to move ahead despite being in excruciating pain. It's certainly about being at the right place at the right time. But doing that also needs a lot of hard work. You need to work hard to understand and master the tricks of your trade. You need to work hard to not just identify but also convert an opportunity. This is something that most entrepreneurs learn and understand over a period of time. But what differentiates a successful entrepreneur from an unsuccessful one is the fact that a successful entrepreneur knows how, when there are no opportunities around, to create one!

Entrepreneurship is years of hard work to mould and improvise our game. It is not a momentary thing. It is more of a continuous process. We need to learn, and unlearn. We need to have the ability to challenge the status quo. We need to know how to question our thoughts for a meatier outcome. It is hard work that helps us understand these things better. But all this cannot negate how luck has been of great help to those around us. Luck does exist. We all know that. But someone's luck can never become our excuse to come to a standstill. It should become our fuel to work harder. People are lucky. And we mostly see luck in its past tense, when it is already out there in the open. And at times, even seasoned entrepreneurs tend to believe that they are behind because the competition is lucky. Well, luck is involuntary. We can't really control it. Also, luck doesn't guarantee the determination an entrepreneur builds with sheer hard work. It doesn't guarantee skill. It comes with its own share of challenges. Those who are plain lucky can only take limited advantage of it. Luck is not in our control. But hard work is. And the ones who work hard, and get luck by their side, know how to make optimum utilization of the invaluable opportunity. They, then, become a lethal combination. Hoping for luck is a great thing. And one should always hope for something so positive. But waiting for luck can be highly disastrous. As entrepreneurs, we are expected to make things happen.

Sometimes hard work is confused with luck. But luck doesn't last forever. Hard work does. And the skill that comes along with hard work does. If luck were enough to make a good leader or an entrepreneur, some really dumb people would be on top. Even though some successful entrepreneurs have mentioned luck as one of the factors that contributed to their success, it was not the only one. No leader ever was just plain lucky, including the ones who were supposedly born with silver spoons. And that's because over a period of time, even these leaders had to perform. They had to prove their mettle. They had to justify the very reason that they are at the top of the ladder. They had to move beyond their legacy. Else, sooner rather than later, they would be out of the game.

Every single phenomenon or success of an entrepreneur that we find unbelievable, we connect it straight with good luck. Every single strategy and outcome that we don't fully understand, we credit it to good luck. Every single accolade that is not yet a part of our story is inclined towards good luck too. But not everything revolves around luck and hard work. There are quite a few things that come in between luck and hard work. These include assumptions, perceptions, and more. When things are way beyond our imagination, and we don't have any answers, we align every such feat to a doubtful maybe. And this maybe is more of an accusation for some wrongdoing. It is a result of our limited world and knowledge. We don't try to dig deeper. When we can't get to a conclusion, we forget about luck and hard work, we just leave it to a maybe. And it slowly becomes a part of our belief system. It puts us back into a zone that can be a big threat to an entrepreneur—the comfort zone.

You can pick up any biography or an autobiography of a legendary leader, and you'll know how they were crazy enough to meet their goals, how they relentlessly worked hard to bring about a change in the world around them. You might find a couple of pages on how they were lucky at times, too. But along with focus, a common thing among all of them was their madness to make a difference. It was their will to achieve their goals. And it was this infectious courage that made people around them align with their so-called impossible vision. And that's exactly the leaf that we can take out of their book, and bring about the difference that we intend to. It is this leaf that will give us enough strength to manoeuvre our ship into a direction that would take us closer to a sunnier tomorrow. It is this tomorrow that translates our vision into reality, and makes sure that the legacy of our good work lives much longer than us.

26) Instincts talk. Listen!

The more you talk, the less you listen.
The less you listen, the more you fault.

It is a known fact that entrepreneurship is not a role that we play for a part of the day. It is a mindset we have, a life we lead!

Today, with the kind of exposure and technology that we have at our disposal, we try to bring down the risk of entrepreneurship substantially. We lose ourselves to the game of evaluation. We are more inclined towards an oxymoron called the safe bet. Well, there is no such thing; if it is really that safe, it is not a bet. But one thing that sets apart a good entrepreneur from a great one is his instinct!

Yes, we all have this capability to know what's good for us. It is that unknown energy inside that tells us what would work for the business and the ecosystem both. However, the difference is that only a few of us pay attention to this great power called instinct. If every entrepreneur would rely on just statistics and research, there would be no innovation. It is only because people heard their instincts right that they could challenge the status quo and take that big leap. It is only because they heard that voice loud and clear they made good use of it for those crucial life-changing decisions.

So it is perfectly all right to not have enough facts to support your next move, provided you can hear that instinct right. How does one connect with one's instinct? Well, here are five simple ways that will help you connect with your instincts better:

Take a Pause: Picture this: you are running a marathon. And in the process you have to hit the bullseye on a dartboard. Seems impossible? Well, that's exactly what happens when you are running around to make both ends meet. That's when a pause, a break, can make a huge difference. This much-needed pause does give you the opportunity to look at the dartboard clearly. That's when you'll at least know what your target clearly looks like.

Zoom Out: With the kind of involvement an entrepreneur has got in the day-to-day activities of his venture, it is almost impossible for him to stay away from it. For an entrepreneur, especially the one who's heading a start-up, detailing is crucial. But what's even more important is to have a zoomed-out perspective to look at the bigger picture. This is when the possibility of an instinct striking you is much higher. It comes in very handy during decision-making.

Disconnect: As much as one gets involved in their business, the word *disconnect* plays a major role in shaping one's thoughts. In fact, to connect better, sometimes it is important to disconnect. This is when you completely move away from your work, though it is difficult for entrepreneurs as they are used to a 'no shift' work style. But the vacuum this disconnection will create will help you get closer to your instincts. It will help you hear those inner thoughts loud and clear.

Practice Solitude: In a world where we're always virtually connected with people, solitude is hardly found. Though people tend to look at it as an abnormal phenomenon, it is a zone that will help you create a higher degree of space. That's where the best of the ideas strike. And that's where instinct is mostly found.

Stay Calm: When you stay out of noise, you'll hear things closer to you louder. And instincts are no different. A calm mind is a result of high control and practice. It is not easy to achieve. But once achieved, it will make space for a lot of new thoughts to pour in. A cluttered mind that's either constantly worried or is running in emotions like anger will never have space to accommodate any new thoughts, or even instincts for that matter.

Though instincts have no specific formula, these simple steps will help you increase the probability of connecting with them like never before.

Printed in the United States
By Bookmasters